Fearless and Connected

The Human Experience

By Targol Pooler

Cover design by Jon Hanzelka

Published by **Native Book Publishing**.
515 South Flower Street, 18th and 19th Floors,
Los Angeles, California, 90071

This book shares the author's personal experiences related to self-experimentation with Psychedelic Mushrooms, Cannabis and Ayahuasca. These medicines are not legal in many parts of the world. The author is not promoting or encouraging the use of these plants and fungi. Rather, they are simply sharing their own experiences and findings for entertainment and informational purposes only. This book is intended for an adult audience, and it is the responsibility of the reader or listener to adhere to local and national laws and regulations surrounding this topic and these medicines. The author and publisher expressly disclaim any liability, loss, or risk, personal or otherwise, that is incurred as a consequence, directly or indirectly, of the contents of this book.

Certain names and locations have been changed in order to protect the anonymity of the characters in this book.

Printed in the United States of America

Dedications

- ❖ To my mom, who taught me to think critically, challenge self-imposed limits, and fearlessly seek growth and learning.
- ❖ To my dad, who taught me to feel music, taste food, hike mountains, swim in the waters of our extraordinary planet, and not take a single breath for granted.
- ❖ To my little sister Tina, who has been my deepest source of love and moral compass. How beautiful it is to be bonded in this way; each of us is an extension of the other.
- ❖ To my partner, Jason, who has been on a shared journey of healing and growth with me for the past decade. What a thrill to do life with someone who shares values and accepts you so completely.
- ❖ To my baby doggos Loki and Bodhi, who have taught me to be a mom and to give and receive love without judgment. I hold you in love, joy and safety in every way I am able.
- ❖ To my dearest friend Dawn, who saw my best parts when I could only see my worst. My heart flows freely as I take your lead on expressing love in the simplest, purest ways.

Introduction

My name is Targol, pronounced Taer'goal, which means fresh flower in Farsi. I am writing this book now because, after forty-two years in this life, I have found my way to peace and fulfillment. My hope is that by reading about my life journey and the lessons I have learned along the way, you will find a thread or two to pull on your own path to living a purposeful life.

I don't claim to have any answers or to be an expert on how to live life. I do, however, think we have built a society full of expectations that don't serve us individually or as a whole. These expectations, which we often adopt without question, lead to judgment, shame, anger, fear, anxiety, isolation, and a general disconnect from all life around us. It seems that we have forgotten that we are conscious in these complex sentient bodies capable of experiencing life through our thoughts, feelings and senses. Instead, we often live on autopilot, following reactive patterns built from these expectations, wondering what it's all for. So what would happen if we took ourselves off of autopilot, and if we wanted to do so, where would we even start? That is what we will explore in this book.

In the following chapters, you will read about my personal life experiences from the perspective of myself at various ages and that of others in my life. I will do my best to share my inner thoughts in the most direct and honest way I am able. I have cross-referenced these stories against old journals and the memories of friends and family where possible. Some of the names have been changed to respect the anonymity of the characters in the story. How I have come to see the world will be incongruent with what we, as a society, consider normal today. This is in large part because I believe that living in accordance with today's societal norms is not conducive to living a fulfilled life. Those who profit from the current model seem just as stressed and lost as those who do not. It seems we are all seeking something that few in modern society have found. Happiness, inner peace, and purpose.

Contents

Part 1 - Once Upon a Time

Chapter 1: The Big Surprise

"When another person makes you suffer, its because he suffers deeply within himself, and his suffering is spilling over. He does not need punishment; he needs help". By **Thích Nhất Hạnh**

I love Adventure Days!!! Dad doesn't work on Sundays, so he fills the car with blankets and jackets, and mom makes sandwiches and packs the cooler, and we set off to explore. We usually go to the beach or park unless it's summertime and the pool is open. This particular Sunday was during springtime, just a few weeks before my tenth birthday. But today was not a normal Sunday. After breakfast, dad told us that he was taking me and my sister Tina to my uncle's house to visit Grandma. What a bummer...

Grandma would occasionally come with us on Adventure Days, but no one seemed to enjoy themselves when she was with us. On those days, Dad ran around, visibly stressed and anxious, trying to bring comfort to his mom. Grandma was perpetually disappointed with everyone and everything. And mom would not talk much. I would watch Mom tuck her giant sunglasses up on her face so we could not see the creases on her forehead or the tears building up in her eyes. Tina and I would run around and climb rocks or build sandcastles and play in the water. It was my job to make sure Tina didn't pick and eat any mushrooms or get into the ocean deeper than her waist. From afar, I would watch the grownups interact with each other. I didn't really care about what they were saying, but I did find their facial expressions and body language interesting. Dad would make jokes, which would sometimes get a smile out of Grandma, but Mom didn't seem to find them funny. When

Grandma would talk, she looked serious and always stared out into nothingness, looking away from Mom and Dad. Then Dad would shake his head, looking frustrated, and Mom would tuck her sunglasses back up her nose.

Today was a different kind of Adventure Day. Instead of exploring the outdoors, Mom was staying home, and we had to go spend time with Grandma. Ugh…fine! We got dressed, said goodbye to Mom, and got in the car. Dad drove for a while. Then we picked Grandma up from my uncle's house. Tina and I asked where we were going, and Dad said it was a surprise. Grandma asked us how we were, and we answered with basic niceties, not really wanting to engage in conversation. Eventually, she left us alone, and Dad and Grandma started talking in their special language. They spoke this language when they didn't want anyone to know what they were saying. After a long car ride, we arrived at the airport. This was exciting! Dad explained that Grandma was going back to Iran for a few months. Grandma would usually spend a few months out of the year in California with either of my dad's two siblings, occasionally seeing us. For the remainder of the year, she was in Iran. This was great news! No Grandma meant happier parents.

Mom and dad were mostly ignoring each other these days, and when they did need to talk, they would pretend to be fine, but it was obvious that they were not. I remember the previous summer when I was in the pool with my cousin. Her parents were yelling at each other right outside the pool. She asked if my parents argued like that and if I was afraid they would get a divorce. I shared that my parents quietly hated each other, and I would love for them to get divorced because I think they both deserve to be happy. I think my parents thought that they were protecting us by trying to hide it. That may have been true for Tina since she was barely seven at the time and for me when I was younger, but not anymore. I remember many times when I would go to the kitchen to grab some water and hear Mom quietly sobbing in the bathroom. I would sit outside the door and listen until she stopped, and then I would go back to the room where the radio was playing music for me and Tina as we played or did our homework. I remember Dad reaching out to touch Mom's back when they stood close to each other and Mom instinctively repelling away. I remember Mom's face when Dad would say he would be home late because he had to check on Grandma and the late-night hushed yet angry-toned discussions they thought I couldn't hear from the bedroom since I should have been sleeping.

So now we are at the airport to send Grandma back to Iran. Maybe Mom will be less sad now. Maybe Dad will come home right after work, and they can watch a movie and laugh like they used to. Grandma had a lot of luggage, so we went in and helped her get checked in. We went through security, and I asked my dad if we needed a ticket to go through this part because I remembered seeing something on TV. He said that because Grandma is older, we can take her all the way to the gate. Tina and I had not been in an airport since she was a few months old and I was three. Neither of us remembered seeing planes up close and in person, and we pointed at them through the large airport windows and oohed and awed at the size of the wings and the number of windows they each had.

When we got to the gate, we sat with Grandma for a bit, and she tried to connect with us, but we didn't really know her or want to know her, so Tina and I mostly talked to each other. Dad was sweating a lot. He went to the bathroom to use the hand dryers to dry out his shirt. When he came back, it was time to board the plane. We stood in line with Grandma, and as we got close to the beginning of the line, Dad said, "Okay, kids, are you ready? This is the Adventure Day surprise! I talked to the pilot, and he is going to take us for a spin." That didn't feel right. Why was Dad looking behind him so much? Why was he sweating so much? Why were there so many suitcases? Did Mom know this was happening? Why was she not with us? I started to panic, and my dad whispered in my ear, BE GOOD.

Here it was. I was trained for this my entire life. On dentist visits: "Be strong for Tina; don't make a scene. BE GOOD". When getting our ears pierced: "Don't make a face; just look normal so Tina doesn't freak out. BE GOOD". During vaccination visits: "Don't react; be brave for Tina. BE GOOD". I thought about it and played out what NOT being good would look like. I can't make a scene. I don't even know how to make a scene. I've never screamed or shouted, and certainly not in public. I don't want everyone looking at me like I'm one of those kids. You know the ones. The ones that mom and dad pointed out to us as they are hanging off their chairs, screaming or crying to get what they want. So maybe I can get someone's attention and ask for help quietly. But what would I say? My dad, who loves me and whom I have no reason not to trust, is taking me on a plane ride, and yes, my mom knows I am with him. Maybe instead, I will ask someone to help me call Mom. Yes, that is a good idea. But we are getting on the plane now. It's too late.

I got on the plane, and Dad buckled us up. Tina looked at me to see how she should react, and I told her "It's okay! Its just a plane". I am not even sure what that meant, but I guess I thought it would work, and it did. She laid back for a bit and held my hand. Then she turned away to look out the window. The plane backed up and left the gate. After a long wait, we returned to the gate and got off the plane. They announced there was something wrong with the plane and that our flight would be delayed. Dad said he was going to go call Mom. I asked to go with him to talk to her. He said no because he only had a few quarters, and it had to be a quick call. He asked that

I help Grandma watch Tina. As I watched him walk away, I thought, Ok, well, he is calling mom. That means I'm probably overreacting. I'm glad I didn't do anything crazy. Dad came back, and shortly after, the plane started boarding again. Dad buckled us up, and Tina fell asleep almost immediately. I looked at my dad, and he smiled at me. I smiled back, but I remember thinking he looked different somehow. Nervous, maybe; I don't know. Maybe I was the one that felt nervous. I wasn't sure exactly what was happening, but I did know for sure that I did not like this surprise. I fell asleep after takeoff and woke up as we were landing in London.

Dad said we were stopping in London for a while. We will get Grandma on a plane and go home. Dad got us happy meals. We rarely ate out, and when we did, it was only for special occasions. I asked Dad what the special occasion was, and he said we were going home. One of his silly jokes, I thought. I went to the restroom at one point, and on the way back, one of the airport workers asked me if I needed help. I wasn't sure if I did. I thought about asking her if I could call my mom, but then I thought she was going to think I was lost and get the police, and it would be a whole thing. I also wasn't sure if I needed money to call Mom, and I didn't want to get my dad in trouble, so I was not sure what to say. So I didn't say anything and walked back to the gate quickly with my head down.

When we boarded the plane, Grandma got on the same plane as us. Ok, now I was fully panicking. None of this made sense. I asked Dad why Grandma was coming home with us, and he said we would drop her off on the way. I didn't know what to do. What was happening? What should I do? BE GOOD over and over in my head. BE GOOD. So I got on the plane feeling nauseous, stressed, and scared. I thought, well, Dad said the plane is going home, so as soon as we see Mom, she will help make sense of things. This surprise will be over soon, and things will go back to normal.

After we landed, I noticed this airport was different. All the directional signs were primarily in another language, and English was written in smaller letters at the bottom of each sign. All the women, including now-Grandma, had scarves covering their hair like women in old movies from the sixties. I heard someone around us speak Farsi, and I said, Dad, they are from Iran. He smiled. Then I heard others speaking Farsi. I realized just then, at that moment, that we were in Iran, and what he meant by saying we were going home was his home, not mine. It was too late to make a scene now. I felt my whole world collapse in on itself. My heart froze, and my brain drowned in fog. Anything I was feeling was now hidden under a heavy blanket of guilt. I did this to Tina. I was Dad's accomplice. How could I be so stupid? How could I let this happen? Mom will never forgive me. Mom will never forgive me. Mom will never forgive me.

The few days after are fuzzy. I remember Tina and I sitting in the corner of the bedroom on our mattress, only leaving the room to eat because of Dad's persistence. We would ask him where Mom was, and he would say she was coming. There was a phone in the house, but it had a plastic cover over the numbers with small openings over each of the numbers. I watched Grandma put her finger in the holes above the numbers, twist the plastic cover and talk on the phone with someone. When she and Dad were not around, I tried to use the phone but I didn't know how. Even if I did, I would not have been able to dial out internationally but my 9-year-old brain did not know that. I was mostly quiet around Dad and Grandma. I was afraid of Grandma, and I was not sure how I felt about Dad. Around Tina, I was silly and weird. I would pretend to be made-up characters with funny voices. It made her laugh and seemed to take her mind off of missing mom.

When we asked when Mom was coming, Dad would say soon. When we asked when we could go home, he would say that this was home, and he would tell us to stop asking so many questions and try to distract us with pastries, toys, books, and clothes. He had broken my trust, so his distractions were not welcome. Tina and I did our best to distract ourselves. Tina had an old doll with her, and I had a stuffed animal. We would make up stories and take these two on adventures. Most of these stories were about siblings who traveled the world to find their mom or about two moms who flew by every window of every house until they found their children. These characters would laugh and cry on these journeys, and we would laugh and cry in support of them. At night, I would hold Tina, kiss her little face, caress her hair, and tell her some of the stories mom would tell us, like the brave ladybug who didn't let life get her down or the fearful elephant who found his courage by leaning on people who loved him. She would correct me if I messed up the story or didn't tell it exactly like Mom did, as she quietly sobbed in my arms and fell asleep. Once she fell asleep, I would cry into my pillow until I passed out.

This went on for days. I don't know exactly how long after, but one day Dad said he was going grocery shopping. We didn't want to be home alone with Grandma, so we went with him. We were at a farmers market when I heard someone shouting, "Targol! Tina!" I didn't recognize the voice, and only my family called me Targol. To everyone else, I was Terry. So, who was this mysterious woman? She came closer. Tina and I looked at each other in confusion. She came over and hugged us super tight and kissed us profusely. Once we got out of her arms, we both hid behind Dad's legs. What was this new surprise? Dad, also looking surprised to see her, told us that she was our Aunt

Shay. Aunt Shay was one of Mom's sisters, whom we had not seen since we left Iran seven years prior. Apparently, she was looking for us in the area since she didn't have Dad's exact address. She talked to Dad for a while. They seemed to be arguing. Eventually, they came to a consensus, and dad said that Aunt Shay was going to come over for tea later, along with Mamanee and Babaee. This was excellent news! I didn't know Aunt Shay, but I did know Mamanee and Babaee. Mamanee is a term used for grandmother in Farsi, and Babaee is for grandfather. Mom's parents would come visit us every other year or so in California. We knew them, we loved them, and they loved us. They would tell us stories and take us to the park when they visited. They also talked to Mom on the phone often, so maybe they would call her for us. Maybe they knew what was going on and would tell us when mom would come to take us home. Finally, some good news!

Later that day, Tina and I sat by the door, taking turns jumping on a chair to look out the peephole. Eventually, a group of people arrived, and Mamanee and Babaee were the first to walk in. We hugged them for a good while as my dad and grandma greeted the rest of them. Tina sat in my lap, and I sat in Mamanee's lap. I closed my eyes and pretended she was my mom for a few seconds. I felt safe in her arms. I asked her if she could call Mom so we could talk to her. She said not yet, but soon. Mamanee distracted us while Babaee, Aunt Shay and her husband talked to Dad and Grandma. It was a welcome distraction that offered a bit of light for the first time in days. After a while, Aunt Shay came over and said that we would all go to her place on Friday and call Mom from there. Friday was two very long days away, but this was good. I could hear it from Mom herself that she was coming to take us home. It also meant I had two days to figure out how I was going to apologize to her for letting this happen. I could not wait to hear her voice. I needed to know she was okay, and even if she was mad at me, it would still be her voice, Mom's voice.

When they were leaving, I asked Mamanee if Tina and I could stay with her and Babaee. She looked at Dad and then back at me and said we had to stay with our dad. I begged Dad to let us go stay with Mamanee, but he would not budge. The next couple of nights, Tina and I barely slept. We whispered to each other most of the night and would go back and forth between giggling and crying. On Friday, we ate breakfast at lightning speed and put on some of the new clothes Dad had bought for us. We pestered Dad forever until he finally got ready and took us to Aunt Shay's house.

When we got there, Dad said that we would call Mom after lunch. He reminded us to BE GOOD. Lunch was torture and lasted forever. Eventually, the plates were in the kitchen, and the leftovers were put away. I asked Mamanee and Aunt Shay if it was time, and Aunt Shay nodded. We followed Aunt Shay into the living room, and she started to dial. Tina asked me if she could go first. I agreed because she was younger, and I had to gather myself before I talked to Mom. I remember feeling like I was an animal in a zoo. Everyone was sitting around the room, and the phone was in the middle of the back wall. Dad, Babaee, Aunt Shay, and her husband were on one side of the room, and Mamanee and my cousin were on the other side. All eyes were on me and Tina; even my cousin's kittens were staring. I thought about asking if we could talk to Mom from the bedroom with a bit more privacy, but I was afraid Dad would say we couldn't call her at all, so I kept my thoughts to myself.

Tina started talking to Mom, and I could hear Mom's voice coming out of the phone. I felt tears rushing down my face. I grabbed some tissues and put the box in front of Tina. I held Tina from behind as she talked to Mom. She was telling mom that I am not as good at telling stories as her, so she should come soon. She cried and asked Mom why she hadn't come with us. I don't know what Mom said, but after a few minutes, Dad asked Tina to pass the phone to me, so she did, but she held onto the cord. I stayed really close to Tina so she could still hear Mom. I heard Mom say my name, and I shakily, through the sobbing, asked her if she was okay and when she was coming. She said she had her ticket and she would be with us in a few weeks. I started to say I was sorry, and before I could finish, Dad said, “That's enough; you will see her soon." Then I heard someone shouting, "NO. YOU SAID I COULD TALK TO MOM AND I'M NOT DONE”. Mamanee grabbed Tina. It took me a few seconds to realize that was me. I was the one shouting. Is that what I sounded like? Where did that even come from? Dad sat back, and I talked to Mom a bit more. Eventually, Mom said we had to hang up because international calls are expensive, and Aunt Shay was paying for this call. She ended with, “Be strong for Tina; I'll be there soon."

It was so good to hear her voice. She didn't sound angry, and I felt relieved that she was actually coming. But I also felt something else. Something new. It was like I felt stronger somehow. I spent a lot of time thinking about what had happened and why I was feeling this way. Was it that I had shouted? No, it wasn't the shouting itself but rather my standing up for myself. Deviating from what was expected of me and redefining what GOOD was. I wondered if I could have used other means instead of shouting to arrive at the same outcome. I decided this was something I wanted to learn how to do well. I had a voice, and my voice had power. I had power!

Chapter 2: A better Life

"The thing is, the belonging that we all desire so much can never be felt as long as the real YOU is living six feet behind the mask that the world is seeing". By **Blake Chalfant from *The Unseen Way* © 2024**

A little over a year after the Islamic revolution in Iran, Iraq invaded Iran, leading to an eight-year war with no shortage of bloodshed and destruction. I was born in 1982, two years after the start of this war. By the time Tina was born in 1985, my parents had set the wheels in motion to move out of the country. Under normal circumstances, they would not have moved away from their friends and family, but war has a way of forcing decisions that one would not make during peaceful times. I have a handful of memories from that time.

I remember Mom's face as she puckered her lips and patiently practiced blowing out candles with me so I would be ready for my first birthday.

I remember my dad's laughter mixed with my giggles as he pushed me on the swing.

I remember my little hand wrapped around my mom's finger as she pointed at a tree in a book while her hair touched my cheek.

I remember Dad whistling songs as I curled up in his lap in a large wooden rocking chair under a warm, fuzzy blanket.

I remember lying down in my grandparents' house, staring at the wooden beams on their ceiling, and running around their garden, naming the colors of their various flowers.

I have one more memory of that time, though I did not realize it was a memory until I was six or seven. When I was a child, there were three specific recurring dreams I had for years. Dreams... well, more like one fantastical dream and two nightmares.

The fantastical dream was of me flying. I would lift myself up outside of my body and see myself asleep on the bed. Then I would fly down to the bottom bunk and see Tina sleeping, often face-up with one leg over the top of the other and the covers bunched up at the bottom of her feet. Then I would fly around the room and out through the door or through a wall, where I would find Mom reading or watching TV. I would then fly out through the living room window and down the stairs around and around the pool before I flew up to the roof of our apartment, where I would float and watch the stars. The mornings after these dreams were always the best mornings. I was ready to take on the world!

The worst of the two recurring nightmares was of an Adventure Day. Sometimes, for Adventure Days, we would go to a marina close by. We would eat fish and chips and play in the arcade. Then, we would walk the pier and watch the sea lions sunbathing on the giant rocks below. In the nightmare, Grandma was with us. I would come out of the arcade to find her and my mom talking on the pier. Grandma would turn around and look at me, then look back at Mom and push her over the railing. I would scream and run toward the edge to find my mom lying breathless on the rocks below, with blood spreading underneath her broken and lifeless body. Sometimes in this dream, I would push my grandmother off in revenge. Sometimes I would get to my mom just to find I wasn't strong enough to hold on to her as she

> slipped out of my little weak hands and fell. The mornings after these dreams, I was usually extra quiet and would hug my mom for a little longer before heading to school.
>
> In the other nightmare, my desperation to do something was replaced with fear of not knowing what was happening or what to do. I was in a dark, cold room, sitting on the floor with my mom next to me. She was squeezing my forearm to comfort me while holding my newborn sister, who was cry-screaming uncontrollably. The whole room felt like fear. I could feel it in the walls, in the air, and inside my bones. Then I heard a haunting whistle ending in a bang loud enough to shake me, and I would wake up in a panic. This nightmare usually kept me up for the rest of the night.

When I was six or seven, my parents took me and Tina out to a large field filled with families settling onto their picnic blankets, getting ready to see Fourth of July fireworks. Tina and I, like most other kids, were excitedly waiting. We saw a few colorful explosions when I heard it; the haunting whistle ending in a bang loud enough to shake me. Instinctually, I got up and ran toward the parking lot as fast as I could. I heard my mom call my name and then my dad as he chased after me. When he caught up with me, he picked me up, held me, and let me cry for a while. When I calmed down enough to speak, I told him about my nightmare. He started to shake and cry as he put me down. He crouched down in front of me and said my dream was a memory of the war that they had fled, hoping to protect us. In my late teens, I revisited this memory with him, and as tears ran down his face, he added:

> One of their friends had invited them to their child's birthday party while Dad was on a business trip. Mom

had decided not to go alone with a toddler and a newborn. That night, there was a bombing, taking with it several of my parents, friends, and their children, including the hosts and attendees of the birthday party.

So my dream ended up being a memory and a sampling of why my parents decided to leave their home to give their kids a better life! They traded in their corporate jobs and middle-class wages in times of war for blue-collar work and a more humble life in times of peace, leaving behind most of their community.

When we arrived in the United States, we stayed with my uncle, my dad's younger brother, for a couple of weeks before we leased an apartment. I remember touring the apartment with my parents. It was a small and dark 1-bedroom apartment. Mom hated it, but Dad convinced her to temporarily move there until they could get jobs and save up for a house. It turns out that if you immigrate to the United States in the eighties with accents and not enough money to own your own business, it's pretty hard to get a job with decent pay. So mom mostly stayed home with us with a few part-time jobs here or there, while dad worked long hours six days a week, mostly at gas stations and convenience stores. That apartment became our home for the next seven years.

During that time, life was pretty routine. We would get up, eat breakfast, get ready, and go to school. After coming home from school, we would do our homework and have exactly one hour to watch TV or play video games. Once the hour was up, it was time to read until dinner. Over dinner, Mom would ask us about our day at school as well as the TV show, video game, and book we consumed. She would ask lots of questions. I didn't realize this at the time, but she was teaching us to think critically about what we consumed while also unleashing our creativity. She would question if there were other ways to think about issues and if we thought the characters in these stories made good decisions. She would ask us how we, in the shoes of the various people in these stories, could have been more compassionate and less harmful. She would give us a lot to think about, so when bedtime came, we would go to bed thinking about her questions and imagining our day, the books, or shows differently than they were. Most nights, I would find myself getting lost in an imaginary world of wizards in forests filled with giant trees and loving animals as my imagination ran away with itself.

On Saturdays, after mom did the laundry and we helped put it all away, we would go volunteer. Mom would say it's important that we give back. We could not donate money, but we could donate our time, our minds, and our healthy bodies. So we would go to a nearby church or organization and sort clothes or canned goods. Mom was spiritual but not religious. She believed in doing good and sharing what we were able. She would say that we live in a world where most people don't have anyone to help them, so we should try to help anyone we can in any way we can as often as we can. It was fun to volunteer. We met new people who also liked to help and serve in this way.

On Adventure Sundays, we would go on explorations. In addition to having fun running around, climbing things, or kicking a soccer ball around, Mom would draw our attention to plants and animals we saw. She would say, “I wonder if we can find them in the book.”. Mom had a book at home that had lots of plants and animals inside. When we came home from our adventures, we would try to find what we had seen in the book. After reading about them, we would try to draw them using the pictures in the book as a guide.

As a child, I didn't yet have enough perspective to realize how rich my life was and how much there was to be grateful for. Instead, I found myself often embarrassed. Kids in school had fancy bikes and new backpacks every year. They had a variety of clothes, markers, and other fun things. I had all the basics, but my parents could not afford to buy us more than we needed. I remember walking around the playground on Halloween, wishing I had one of the cool store-bought costumes like other kids. Instead, my mom made me an angel costume out of her wedding dress so I could feel included. It's really interesting to look back at this memory now. What is more generous and kind than alternating one's own wedding dress to make a unique and beautiful dress for a child who was also unique and beautiful though didn't know it at the time? Especially when all that child saw was an uncool hand-me-down outfit and an unappreciated gesture.

Because we lived in a small apartment, my mom was not comfortable with us inviting friends over. We were also not allowed to go to our friend's house because mom didn't know their parents and wanted us to be safe. But Mom and Dad never came to school events, so how could they know the other parents? I remember performing Jingle Bells in front of the whole school. I was supposed to play the piano while another kid took the lead on vocals. When the other girl got sick and could not perform, I bravely volunteered to take her place. I was terrified and unsure why I offered to sing and play, and I wasn't sure if I could do it, but I did, and the auditorium buzzed with cheering people. I, however, was holding back tears because I knew both my parents were working that day. Still, I looked out at the sea of kids and parents in the hope that I would find them there.

I wanted what I considered at the time a “normal” life. I wanted to go to slumber parties and join the Girl Scouts. But even setting aside the protective parenting and the financial constraints, I was not exactly a popular kid with a ton of friends. I rejected exactly zero slumber party invites because that was how many I was invited to. On Valentine's Day, every year, our class would make cards for their friends. I would give out at least ten cards to kids I wanted to be friends with and receive only one card each year from my teacher.

Between an unpronounceable name, hairy legs, and being one of a handful of non-white kids in the school, I was an easy target for bullying. I was the last to get picked in sports, even though I was pretty athletic. Kids called me names, pulled on my hair, and made jokes about me being poor. I always had pencil marks on the side of my hand because I was a lefty, and somehow, I was always the only lefty in my class. I was also the first to stand up for other kids who were bullied, which made me even more of a target. I never stood up for myself, and I think subconsciously, I believed I didn't matter as much as the other kids or that I could handle it, so it was fine. I had read in my books about heroes who sacrificed themselves for others, so I think that may have started a thought pattern in me that to be good, I had to sacrifice myself.

At the beginning of the school year, my second-grade teacher asked me if it would be okay if she called me Terry so I would not get picked on as much. I agreed, and for the past thirty-five years, outside of my family, I have been known almost exclusively as Terry. She also asked me if I would be willing to try writing with my right hand. I tried for a few months, and it was not bad, but it slowed me down, and I felt more comfortable with my left, so I switched back by the end of the year. I think about Mrs. M a lot. She was a kind teacher and did her best to help me. I now understand that changing myself to be accepted was not the best approach. She thought that it was and passed on that pattern to me without either of us critically thinking about better ways, like learning about and celebrating our differences for example.

Despite the challenges, I loved school. It was where I could find books to read and problems to solve. I had a few short-lived friendships over the years. In second grade, I became friends with Sam. He was smart and kind and had a killer imagination. He was in a wheelchair, so he would get bullied too. I protected him, and he protected me. We both loved to read and create stories, so we became quick friends and spent most of our recess hours in the library, away from the playground kids. We had tons of fun together until his mom got a job in another state, and they moved.

In the third grade, I met Kelly. She was slim with blue eyes and blond hair. She was beautiful! When she smiled, people would pay attention to what she was about to say or do. She mostly ignored the other kids and liked to hang out with me. She said I looked exotic, and she would style my hair as I read to her. Kelly was never hungry and barely ate anything. If she did nibble on something, she would quickly get sick and throw it all up. I didn't understand it, but I accepted her as she was, and she accepted me. Halfway through the school year, she made some new friends. They were a year older than us and were also slim and beautiful. They would talk about music, TV shows, and boys. She invited me into their group, and at first, I tried to fit in by laughing at jokes I did not understand or letting Kelly dress me up before we met up with them. But I felt like I was lying. I was not into boys yet and did not know any of the bands or shows they talked about. I also didn't feel beautiful enough to be part of that group and thought that they were nice to me out of pity, so I decided to spend more time in the library alone.

Halfway through fourth grade, I met Mica. She had just moved to California from Puerto Rico. I met her one day as we waited for our parents to pick us up. We were in the same grade but in different classes. Mica had black hair like mine, except that mine was wavy and hers was straight. She had bangs, glasses, and braces. She was beautiful! She liked to play sports, so she gave me a reason to spend some recess hours in the playground with her. I had a lot of fun with her and learned that I enjoyed being active in group settings when I felt safe to do so. We were both nimble and flexible, and we talked about becoming gymnasts and traveling the world together. On the last day of fourth grade, she asked me if I knew how to kiss. I did not, and I had not thought about it until then. She asked if I would be willing to practice with her, so we are ready when boys want to kiss us. I had no interest in kissing anyone, but I thought practicing couldn't hurt. We went into a bathroom stall together. She touched my face, and then she kissed me. She tried to stick her tongue in my mouth, and I pulled away. She asked me what I thought, so I shared that her lips were cold and that I didn't want her tongue in my mouth. She started shaking and looked like she was going to cry. She ran out of the stall, and fourth grade was over. I tried to talk to her after the summer when school started again. She said some mean things to me in front of other kids. I don't remember exactly what she said, but I remember feeling hurt and embarrassed. We never talked again.

At home, we didn't really talk about our feelings. Mom challenged our logical brains to think, learn, and stretch, but when it came to emotions, there was no room for them. Dad was mostly working and not around, and Mom was generally either patient and loving, or she was sad. When she was patient and loving, and we came to her with big feelings, she would ask questions and help us logically break down what we were feeling and why. When she was sad, it was like her body was there, but she was not. If we disrupted her when she was like that, Mom would either get annoyed with us and ask us to go to our room and play, or she would shake it off and pretend to be okay. When I would ask her why she was sad, she would deny it as if there was no sadness to talk about. So, I learned to try my best to logically work through my feelings, and when I could not, I would pretend not to feel them until I did not feel them anymore. I remember the first time I saw Star Trek; it was like the world finally made sense. I figured we were Vulcans. Intelligent, logical beings who find emotions tedious and unnecessary.

Outside of the few friendships I mentioned, I was mostly alone. I spent as much time as I could in the library. In the library, I was well liked. Our elementary school shared a library with the middle school and high school next door. First the middle schoolers and then the high schoolers realized that I was more than happy to help do their homework for them, for ice cream money. So they would line up with a quarter or two in hand, and I would choose which assignments of theirs I wanted to do. My favorite topics were mathematics and the sciences. By the end of the fourth grade, I had solved all of the math problems in the high school textbooks. This also meant I had plenty of quarters to share with my class on Wednesdays when we had ice cream sandwiches for sale during recess. I had found this to be the key to my surviving school.

One day in 5th grade, one of the older kids came to our class with a note. She struggled to read the name on the note, so she handed it to my teacher. My teacher looked at me and said I was needed in the principal's office. Oh no, they knew, I thought. My world was about to end. I slowly peeled myself off the chair and walked on my wobbly legs toward the door with my head down, trying to hold back tears. I felt faint, but I pushed through and followed the older kid across the yard to the principal's office. I walked in, and my mom was sitting there with the principal, vice principal, and a man and woman I did not recognize. The people I did not recognize were in suits, and I thought, oh no, the FBI is here to arrest me for doing the high schooler's homework. I'm toast!

I was asked to sit next to my mom, so I did. I was shaking my leg, so my mom put her hand on my leg to calm me. The vice principal asked me if I remembered taking all those tests earlier in the year. I did, in fact, remember. They had the whole school participate in two full days of tests outside of our classroom schedule. Those tests were both challenging and interesting, and I had a lot of fun taking them. When I told them that I remembered the tests, that I had really enjoyed taking them, and that I wished the school had more tests like that, they laughed. I thought I said something wrong so I told myself repeatedly internally to shut up and to stop being weird.

The woman in the suit shared that those tests were to assess kids all across the United States so they could find high-potential children. She shared that I had scored high in most categories, especially math and science, and that they wanted to talk to me and my parents about putting me in a special program for genius children. She explained that the plan included me taking an expedited course over the summer to test out of middle school and high school so I could go to college the following year. This sounded too good to be true. My eyes lit up, and I asked if there would be more books in the library of this college and other students that enjoyed learning. They laughed again and said that there would be more books than I could read and most of the students in this school were there to learn but that they would be much older than me. The University I would attend, was an Ivy League School and they explained that the process to get in is rigorous and that I would have to work hard over the summer to get ready for the program. That sounded like a very welcome challenge. I looked over at my mom. She did not look excited. They handed Mom some papers as they explained there would be no cost to her and that I would be covered through a full scholarship. Mom put the papers in her purse and told them that she would talk it over with my dad.

When we left the principal's office, I pleaded with her desperately to accept on the spot, and she said, BE GOOD. So, I stopped myself from making a scene, and I walked with her to the car. On the ride home, we were quiet. I tried talking about it, but she told me if I kept asking, the answer would be no, so I stopped pestering her. That night, I couldn't sleep, so I stayed up with my ear to the wall. Eventually, Dad came home, and they talked about it while he ate. She said she doesn't want me to miss out on my childhood and does not think it's a good idea. He said that not being challenged in school is torture, and if it's something I want to do, then they should consider the opportunity. Their discussion turned into an argument and went in circles for a while. Eventually, they stopped talking, and I cried myself to sleep. In the morning, I asked mom, and she said that for now, the answer is no, and if it changes, she will tell me and that I should stop asking. And that was that. That was the last time we talked about it. A month or so later, dad had a surprise for us on Adventure Day. We were going to go see Grandma before she left for Iran.

Chapter 3: In Limbo

"The truth is the truth, whether or not it is accepted by the majority. Therefore, I tell you children, it takes great courage to stand up for and protect what is right". By **Thích Nhất Hạnh**

That first month back in Iran was confusing. After that Friday at Aunt Shay's, we had a few weeks before mom would arrive. Dad decided to take us to the north of Iran, where we could enjoy some forest hikes and beach time. We stayed with Grandma's sister, Aunt May. She was kind and not at all like her sister. She had a farm with tons of animals for us to interact with and plenty of chores to keep us busy. We helped feed the chickens and milk the goats. We chased the ducks, and the dogs chased us. We were there for about a week, and it was a welcome distraction.

Knowing mom was coming soon, helped me and Tina enjoy our time at the farm. Aunt May cooked delicious food for us, and she wore colorful clothing. The food she cooked was local to where she lived and where she grew up so it was different than mom's cooking. It was really fun to cook with her and learn about different ways of preparing food and cooking with vegetables I was not familiar with. Aunt May would give us fresh milk form her animal companions and fruit from her trees as she taught us about farm life. She had never married and lived with her longtime friend. Those two ladies took care of each other like a married couple in love. Neither had children, and the farm animals were very much like their children. They cared for them compassionately and patiently, as any good parent would. Aunt May reminded me of my mom. She was strong and vocal about her beliefs, even if that meant speaking on behalf of my mom when Grandma was unkind in her choice of words. She had no problem standing up to her sister and sharing her perspective. She seemed fair, brave, and kind. I instantly became a fan of hers and could not wait to tell Mom all about her. She also made my tenth birthday as special as possible, considering the circumstances. I think I had three different birthday celebrations in a span of two weeks. One at Aunt May's farm. One back in Tehran at Aunt Shay's. And another at Mamanee and Babaee's house after mom arrived.

After a really nice time visiting with Aunt May, we came back to Tehran, and Dad enrolled us in a public school. In Iran, when you come from a foreign country, you have to test out of each grade to start at the appropriate level in school. Given that neither Tina nor I could read or write, that meant we had to start in the first grade. So, just like that, my label changed from child genius to illiterate giant. Tina was only a year older than the first graders, so she was quick to make friends. For me, it was unbearable.

In addition to the guilt, fear, hurt, and confusion from recent events, I had now also lost my identity. If I was not the smart kid, who was I? If I couldn't even read a basic children's book, what was the point of living at all? If it were not for Tina and the promise of Mom coming, I would have taken my life. Over the next few years, I spent a lot of time thinking about how and where I would do it, and I had a few options lined up just in case.

In addition to being a ten-year-old kid sitting in a first grade classroom, the school itself was a shock. An all-girls public school with uniforms that consisted of long-sleeved robes, full-length pants, black shoes, and a maghnae. A maghnae is fabric sewn such that you pull it over your head and place the elastic cord behind your neck to ensure only your face is visible through it, covering your hair, ears, and neck. This uniform fully erases any form of expression, which I guess is the whole point of a uniform. I had no understanding of cultural norms and the copious amount of etiquette expected of girls. The school year was also nearing end, so I just showed up to school, made zero effort, and tried my best to stay out of everyone's way until mom arrived.

When the day came, despite my begging and pleading, dad decided it was best that Mamanee and Babaee picked mom up from the airport. Mom would land in the early hours of the morning, and he promised he would take us to see her after breakfast. Tina and I were up all night, fully clothed, ready to go as soon as dad was willing to take us. We left right after breakfast. When we knocked on the door, and Mom was there, it took me a second to process what I was seeing. Mom looked like she had not eaten for weeks; her hair was frazzled; she had bruises all over her arms and shoulders, which she was clearly trying to keep covered with a cardigan that looked two sizes too big on her. Tina jumped in her arms, and I followed. We held each other and cried for several minutes before going to her bedroom, where we sat on her bed and continued to cuddle and cry for a while longer.

Tina would not let go of Mom. She couldn't. Mom held her, stroked her hair, kissed her little head, and said over and over again, “I love you; I missed you so much." I just laid there on top of mom and smelled her skin. How can you miss how someone smells so much? It was really her. It felt so good to be in her arms and hear her voice. She asked what we had been doing, and Tina and I told her about the farm and Aunt May. Then I told her about school, and she was so visibly upset that she had to take a few deep breaths to calm herself. Weeks earlier, she had not wanted me to join the expedited learning program because she didn't want me to grow up too fast. That ship had sailed, and now her concern was me falling behind. She told me not to worry and that she would figure something out. She added that I would not have to go back to the 1st grade.

When Tina went to help Mamanee set the table, I asked Mom when we were going home, and she looked surprised, not realizing that this whole time, we didn't connect the dots and that there was no going back. At least not for years, and that is only if we were lucky. Dad's little brother, whom we had stayed with when we first moved to the U.S., had applied for permanent residence for us. Cases like this one usually take ten to twenty years, depending on what state you apply from, your country of origin, and the circumstances of the application. Mom explained that we would be here until our green cards were ready. It could take years before we can go back. She also added that she and Dad would be getting divorced. She explained that in Iran, fathers get full custody of the children and added that Dad has agreed to let us stay with her over the weekends. She said we would have to learn to adapt to this culture and that this would be our home for the foreseeable future. I pretended to understand, but inside, I was a spiraling mess. I could feel myself unraveling. I wanted to cry but wanted to be strong for Mom. I wanted to scream, but I didn't want to scare Tina. I wanted to run until my body couldn't, but I didn't want to move away from Mom's smell and heartbeat. I am not sure how long after I accepted this reality, or even if I ever fully did accept it. I was in limbo, waiting with no control over when my life could resume.

While Mamanee kept Tina busy, I asked Mom if she was okay. I asked about her bruises. She explained that she had to get rid of all of our stuff and move everything around by herself with no help. She added that she did not know where we were for the first few days until she got a call from Aunt Shay, who had found us, and that she had gotten very sick. She shared that she called Dad's siblings to find out if they knew anything. My aunt knew nothing, but my uncle, after two days of Mom calling hospitals and morgues, told her that Dad had taken us to Iran and that she should check the mailbox. Dad had left her a letter and an airline ticket. I later found out that he had also hidden her phone book to buy himself some time to get settled. Luckily, Aunt Shay, who had recently moved, had given Mom her new number just a couple of days before the big surprise, and Mom had written down her new number on the back of a tissue box. She called Aunt Shay immediately after talking to my uncle and asked her to look for us in the area.

I didn't like anything I was hearing, but I was thankful she was trusting me with the truth. I finally understood what had happened. Dad kidnapped us, brought us to Iran so he could have full custody of us, and left her behind to decide if she would join us or not. She, of course, joined to be near her kids, and we were stuck in Iran indefinitely. A nightmare that I couldn't wake up from. I kept repeating her words to myself. I will have to adapt. I will have to learn to live here. I will have to adapt. I will have to learn to live here.

Mom didn't seem to sound mad at me like I had expected that she would. I apologized to her for letting dad take Tina and not stopping it from happening. She looked surprised and told me that I was also a victim of his choice and that none of this was my fault. I, of course, knew she was only trying to make me feel better and that I was, in fact, very guilty and ashamed.

We all ate lunch together: Mom, Tina, Mamanee, Babaee, and me. I kept looking at the clock because I knew Dad would come to pick us up soon, and I was dreading having to leave. Mom caught me looking at the time and said:

> Let's enjoy every moment we have together and not waste it in fear of it ending. We are here now, safe and among loved ones. Let's enjoy the present moment.

After lunch, Dad came to take us home. We begged him to let us stay the night, but he refused. I was realizing he had all the power, and the rest of us had to do what he said. I wondered if that would ever change.

Dad told us that we could stay with Mom every weekend which in Iran is Thursday and Friday. The weekend was 2 days away, so Tina and I quickly agreed in fear that he would change his mind. After that, we stayed with Mamanee for a few minutes, and Mom and Dad talked in the other room. The next day, we did not go to school, and by the end of the week, Mom had found a private school that specializes in helping foreign kids adapt to the cultural norms of Iran, and catch up in school. The school year was at its end, so we had about one hundred summer days to learn as much as we could and test out of as many grades as possible.

After enrolling in school, Dad agreed to let us go to Mom's every day after school so she and Aunt Shay, who was a math teacher, could help us study. Some days, Mom would work with me and Aunt Shay with Tina, and some days, vice versa. It was exhausting work for everyone involved. We had a long-packed study schedule to the point where even bio breaks and snack breaks were paired with quizzes. There was no time to waste. Even though they did math a bit differently than in the U.S., math and sciences were the easy parts. The classes in which I had no base knowledge were quite difficult like geography, history, and religious studies. I'm sure if we were going at a slower pace, learning about some of these topics would have been interesting, but because of the condensed schedule, we just had to memorize everything and move on to the next topic.

There was no time to imagine or daydream. There was no time to live in the shoes of the characters or explore the mountains and rivers in these books. So we crammed, crammed, and crammed.

Before we knew it, it was time to take the tests. Tina passed her 2nd-grade exams with flying colors, so she was back on track and could start third grade the following week as the school year started. I passed through the first five grades, scoring low only in spelling. Given the circumstances and my exceptional grades otherwise, the school gave me a pass so I, too, could pick up where I left off. The first obstacle has been completed. Now, we had one week to relax before starting public school. The private school was very expensive, so going there for the following year was not an option. I knew I was not ready for public school, but I had no choice.

Tina had some struggles, but she fit in better than I did and seemed to enjoy going to school. She made friends very quickly and adapted well. It was different for me. I was older, so I was expected to know how things worked. Instead, everything I would say or do seemed to be taken as some kind of insult. I was quickly branded as the Disrespectful American Kid and had no idea how to be anything else. By the end of my first week in school, I had been expelled for the first time. I raised my hand in class and asked a question. My question was worded in such a way that my teacher thought I was being sarcastic and insulting. I was sent home and told not to come back. As soon as I got home, I called Mom and told her what had happened. She told me that she would take care of it, and the next morning, she came over and took me to school. She explained to my teachers and school administrators that I was raised in a different culture and that it would take time for me to adapt. She reminded them that it was their job to compassionately show me the way. After that, I tried even harder not to be disruptive, but no matter what I did or didn't do, my actions were often perceived differently than I intended.

On top of all of this, the elastic cord on the back of my maghnae was giving my neck a rash, so I cut it. This meant it would slide back and show a bit of my hair. This was taken as an intentional act of rebellion by the Disrespectful American Kid. The truth is, this did not start as an act of rebellion but rather as seeking some form of comfort as I struggled through the day. After a while, other girls started choosing comfort over expectations, and before I knew it, half the school was wearing their maghnae as I did. I found this inspiring and felt less alone. Then, I started to push the limits of our dress code further. I wore colorful socks and hemmed my pants about an inch shorter, so when I walked, you could see flashes of color from my intentionally unmatched socks. I was stopped in the hallways often to explain what had happened. I would say that I grew taller and could not afford new pants. Eventually, they gave me a new pair of pants, and I quickly hit a growth spurt, as did several other girls in the school. Then I started to roll up my sleeves to two-thirds length, showing my wrists, and that also became a trend. The more of us participated in these acts of rebellion, the less we would get into trouble with the school.

I realized there is power in numbers and value in community. I found it easy to make friends at this point because most of the girls thought it was cool to be like the Disrespectful American Kid. I had also lost my crippling fear of getting in trouble. I felt empowered by my rebellious friends, so I pushed harder. I love to sing, but singing is illegal in Iran, especially for women, with one exception: choir. I joined the school choir so I could sing religious prayers. The girls who joined choir at the time were followers of Islam and respected the rules. We were allowed to sing the prayers calmly, in a respectful tone, quietly enough so that no one outside of the school would hear. I was not a follower of Islam, nor did I see logic in these rules, so the first time I was able to take the lead on a prayer during our morning assembly, I turned the microphone up. Way up, and I sang the prayer as loudly and creatively as I could. It felt like the whole school cheered when I was done. Surprisingly, my choir teacher was equally cheerful and enjoyed the performance, but the school administration was not pleased, so I got suspended.

During my suspension, other girls in the choir performed the prayers, singing their hearts out. A couple of them also got suspended, but eventually, the school realized they could not control this movement, and they addressed only the most egregious of acts. Like when I shaved my legs for gym class. This was not just a school rule but an unlawful act if the woman or girl was unwed when taking this action. Mom would smooth things over at school when things got too heated. I did witness one interaction where she reminded them that before the revolution, they were all walking around in crop tops and miniskirts, so they knew better than to terrorize young girls about silly things that have now become law. She refocused them on our education and reminded them that it was their job to focus on school-related topics and the parent's job to teach us about our virtues and values in life.

I wish I could say I was intentionally and selflessly an activist with the goal of driving change. But at this point in my life, I was a traumatized pre-teen who didn't care about consequences, so these small acts of rebellion gave me something meaningful to care about. I found it incredibly inspiring that there were so many girls around me who also wanted to express themselves and break out of their socially conditioned chains. We were powerful together and could not be controlled as easily. Our voices commanded attention as we sang for ourselves and each other. It's heartbreaking that these events happened roughly thirty years ago, and girls and women in Iran are still fighting for a modicum of freedom.

It felt good to not feel alone with these thoughts. By the time I entered my teenage years, I would talk openly with the girls and some teachers about how different life was in the United States. My perspective was valued, and they had so many questions. They would bring books and articles for me to translate and make sense of. I made many friends during this time, and the closest of them was Maryam. She and her twin sister, Zahra, were in choir. Zahra was a follower of Islam and all of its strict laws. Maryam was a free spirit who wanted to study abroad and see the world. She was curious about all cultures and was very well-read, so we had a lot to talk about. Zahra cautioned Maryam about becoming my friend. She would say that I would corrupt her and lead to her death.

Maryam did not listen to her sister, and we quickly became the closest of friends. At school, we would study together, eat together, play the same sports, read the same books, and sing together. We would then walk home together, while Zahra would walk on the other side of the street to protect herself from my Western ways. When we would laugh loud enough that Zahra could hear us, she would cross the street to reprimand us, and that of course would make us laugh harder. Like Zahra, their parents were strict followers of Islam. They were already in search of marriage prospects for their girls in preparation for high school graduation. College was out of the question, and the girls, of course, did not have a say in the matter.

Maryam would tell me about her plans to run away and flee the country. We joked about leaving together and starting a life somewhere new. I had my mom to fight for me; she had no one. She was alone in this world. She often talked about feeling like a puppet, watching her parents pull her strings. She had been tutoring girls at school and had money saved up for her great escape. She was determined and had a plan. She had connected with some girls in Turkey who had offered to give her a place to stay if she made it out there. I warned her that this could be a sex trafficking situation for all we knew. She didn't care. She wanted out, and she was determined to write her own story.

Right before graduation, Zahra found Maryam's stash of cash and told their parents. Her parents let her know that she would be married right after graduation to a man of their choosing, so Maryam, determined to live as she wanted, took her own life. Her sister Zahra found her body along with a letter addressed to Zahra encouraging her to choose the life she wants, not the life that is expected of her. Maryam wanted to write her own story and understood that sometimes the cost of inspiring change is unbelievable courage and heartbreaking sacrifice. Change is not easy, but it is necessary for us to grow and evolve as individuals and communities. Maryam chose death over an unwanted life forced upon her. She did not have to die, but her death resulted in at least four of our friends that I know of going to college and building careers before families. Among these girls was Maryam's sister, Zahra. She convinced her parents, in honor of her sister, to allow her to choose her life. Last I heard, she had obtained a PHD in chemistry and lived in Europe with her chosen husband and twin daughters.

During the year I took off after high school. I had been in Iran now for eight years, and there was still no word about our green card application. It had been fourteen years since my uncle applied for us, so I decided to write a heartfelt letter to the U.S. Department of Immigration for consideration of expediting the case. I never heard back. I had not given up, but I was now eighteen and only had a few years before I was no longer eligible. Once I turned 21, I would no longer be a minor under my dad's care and would have lost my chance to come back home.

Additionally, Maryam's death weighed heavily on my heart. If the Disrespectful American Kid had not come into her life, maybe she could be alive. On the outside, I would smile and engage in normal pleasantries. On the inside, I was sinking into a black hole, desperately trying to catch my breath. Have you ever tried to take a deep breath and it feels like you can't get enough air into your lungs to be able to actually breathe? At this point in my life, I had not yet gone to therapy. I was still emotionally suppressed, and my thoughts about all that had happened in my eighteen years were mine alone. I remember Maryam sharing that a cousin of hers, who had gone to therapy, used journaling as a means to process their trauma. Maryam also shared that she had tried it and found it useful. She would write down her thoughts and burn the pages so there would be no evidence to be used against her.

I took a year off after high school and spent most of my time at Dad's. He had recently moved to a small town two hours outside of Tehran. This town had mountains on one side, a forest on the other, and a windey river running through. It was beautiful and peaceful. Tina was still in school, so she stayed with mom, and we saw each other every other weekend when I drove back to the city to visit. It was the first time Tina and I were separated. It was the first time in my life that I shifted from thinking about Tina and her well-being to my own. What was I going to do with my life? What was my plan if I had to stay in Iran? Did I want to go to college? What kind of job would I want? Who did I want to be in this world? What were my options?

I don't say this lightly; staying there with dad, and journaling saved my life. It was a small town where the gossip game was strong, and I had no interest in that. Though I was occasionally the source of gossip since I would drive myself to and from the city, walk the trails sometimes without Dad, and I would talk out-loud to the plants and wildlife. When I was not frolicking around without male supervision, as the locals described it, I was writing. I started by writing fantasy adventures, rekindling my childhood imagination, and finding strength through the stories of the characters who were stranded in lands far away as they bravely navigated the world around them until they found their way out of limbo. I would write about the trees, cranes, and turtles I interacted with on my walks. And eventually I started writing about what had happened that resulted in us being in Iran. I cried for the nine-year-old girl and was able to see the story from a fresh perspective. Mom had been right all along. I was just a kid and was not at all at fault for my dad's decision. I was also more resilient than I thought I was. Everything that I had lived through, fought through, and learned through made me stronger and less afraid of what may happen next.

As I let go of some of the guilt and shame, I decided to start studying for the college exams. In Iran, the interest in going to college far outweighs the available capacity, so the college exams narrow down who is qualified and for what universities and majors. I chose math, physics, and chemistry as my top 3 choices and took the exams twice. The first time, I did not pass. The second time, I was accepted into my top-choice of university to study physics. I was not yet at peace with the possibility of having to stay in Iran, but I did need a plan, and going to college made sense. So, I started school in the fall.

College was co-ed, and my rebellious nature grew as I challenged where women were allowed to sit in the classroom, which door we could use to enter campus, what times we had access to professor office hours, and even how we were graded. During my first year in college, I led several protests and was widely supported by both students and professors. We forced the administration to update some of their dated policies. I had decided that if I had to live there for any amount of time, I had to try to make it more palatable, and if I got arrested or killed for trying to drive positive change, that was an acceptable outcome. It sounds noble and inspiring, but really, it was what I needed to do to survive. I had seen a different way of living, so I knew life did not have to be that way. As I saw it, it was my responsibility to share that knowledge and empower others to stand up for themselves as I did for myself. Daring to question and push against unfair and illogical boundaries was necessary, and not doing so was not really an option for me. I also fought for Maryam. The Disrespectful American Kid who led her down this path owed it to her to fight for all the Maryams out there.

After my second semester, the long-awaited letter from the U.S. immigration department arrived. Our case was ready for review. Great news, kind of, but also kind of not. Since Mom and Dad were divorced and Dad's brother had applied for us, Mom was no longer on the case. So this meant Dad, Tina, and I could get interviewed and hopefully come back home, but mom had to stay in Iran. How do you find peace with leaving your mom yet again, this time by choice, not knowing when you will be reunited next? How do you willingly rip her two girls away from her again, leaving her behind with no immediate way to join?

Chapter 4: Fearless

your fears
are brown needles
tangled up with what's
still green and living
all you have to do
is reach out, touch them
and watch them lie like
death in the dust

"Brown Needles" by Patrick Merle Sellin, from *My Soul To Keep* © 2023

Shoukou, a young girl in her early teens, lived in a small town in the north of Iran by the Caspian Sea. She loved going to the beach and dancing in the sand as she collected pebbles and shells. She loved visiting with her grandmother and learning about different plants and how they could be used to heal the human body and mind. Shoukou lived during a time when societal norms dictated that instead of going to school, as soon as girls got their menses, it was time to get married and raise as many babies as their bodies allow. She was married off to a forty-something-year-old military officer, and they had two children. She thought herself lucky because her husband would be away for many months at a time. While he was away, she learned how to read and gained access to books. She would go on adventures with the characters in these stories, and one book at a time, her perspective on what was possible in this world grew.

When Shoukou was twenty, the plague ran through her town, taking with it many people, including her husband. In cases like hers, it's common for the young woman's parents to quickly find a new husband to take care of her and her children. However, Shoukou had no intention of living a life that was pre-written for her. As her perspective grew and her reality expanded, she decided that she would choose her life and not stand by and watch life just happen to her. In her books, she had read about warriors and people who traveled the world. She learned about different trades and about love. If all this was possible for the people in her books, why not for her as well? After all, she was no less smart, capable, or determined to live a full life.

So when her husband passed, it was time to set her fears aside and find her way. She rejected her parents' financial help, which came with the expectation of a marriage of their choosing. Instead, she supported herself and her children by making and selling clothing. She was taught at a young age how to sew, and she had received enough praise from her friends and neighbors for the clothing she created and wore that she knew this skill could provide her with options in life. So she started by making clothes for friends at a low cost and then for friends of friends, and before she knew it, everyone in town wanted to have a Shokou-made garment.

Within a year of her husband's passing, she caught the attention of a young man who was no more than eighteen years old. He had surpassed the expectations of his age academically and was already an officer in the army. He was intelligent and kind, as well as handsome and charming like the gentlemen she read about in her books. They quickly became infatuated with each other and fell completely in love. It was not easy to choose a life outside of what was considered normal at the time. They were shamed and isolated from their community. But neither regretted choosing a life together.

After they married, she continued to work as a seamstress, and she paid for him to continue his education until he was fluent in several languages and completed his Master's Degree in Criminal Investigation. Her income exceeded his, so they lived comfortably above what was possible for most military families of their rank. They had four children together, and he raised all six children as his own. Over the years, he worked his way up the ranks until he became a general in the Shah's army while she grew her business, traveled the world, and continued her education by reading at least one hour daily, without exception.

Shoukou, or, as I knew her, Mamanee, was a creature of routine. Her routine changed over the years as she transitioned from one life stage to another. When I was in my early teens, her routine was as follows: she would wake up and do what we would classify as yoga today for thirty minutes. Then, she would shower, put on a snazzy outfit of her own creation, and eat a simple breakfast. She would run her errands before lunch, come home to eat with Babaee, and then power walk from one end of the bedroom to the opposite end of the living room, counting her steps to make sure she got the desired activity. She would then read for an hour or more and take a nap. After her nap, she would spend time with Babaee watching television, which, truthfully, was more them talking and laughing among themselves than watching television. Then they would eat dinner and say goodnight to each other as they held each other for at least thirty seconds, then kiss for even longer before she went to her room, where she would change and curl up in bed with a book.

I remember that there was always one book on the bedside table right under her reading glasses and another book on the floor next to the table, ready to go as soon as she finished the one she was reading. She would use a clean folded tissue to hold her page and have a tissue box nearby in case the book evoked tears. The entire wall behind her 12-person dining table was a bookcase with a wide array of books. I remember many of them, as I spent my teenage years reading books of her choosing as well as my own to expand my young mind. Memoirs, romantic novels, world history, fiction, philosophy, psychology, and even theology. My grandmother considered herself a non-religious, spiritual Muslim. When I inquired about the Bible, I saw on her bedside table, she told me that she has read several versions of the Bible, Torah, Quran, and many books on Buddhism, Zoroastrianism, and many other religions more than once. When I asked her why, she said

> "Anything you read has something to offer about how to live a fulfilling life. Through the stories, no matter the topic or genre, you can think about who you want to be and how you want to show up in this world. None of us are born to be as we are at any given moment; rather, we are meant to learn from our own stories and those of others so that we can grow and become better versions of ourselves from moment to moment."

Babaee's happiness seemed to come from Mamanee's happiness. She was a free spirit and traveled the world. Every year or two, she would go to a new place and come back with stories about the culture, food, fashion, and people. He would occasionally join, but often work and kids would keep him home. He missed his love when she was gone. She would call routinely, and they would talk and giggle on the phone like teenagers. He would light up when she would say she was homebound soon.

When I was eight, Babaee took me to the park, and as he was pushing me on the swing, I asked him if he was happy in life. He said,

> Every moment we get to live is a gift, and every one of those moments that I get to be with someone I love is a sacred moment. Not everyone gets to love or be loved. I get both from Mamanee, my kids, and my grandkids. That means every moment of every day is a good one.

Like all couples, they had their disagreements, but they never stayed mad at each other for more than a few minutes. He would grab her and apologize, or she would. It didn't seem to matter who was at fault or what the disagreement was about. What seemed to matter more was their desire to forgive and simply live in love. After fifty years of marriage, Shoukou and Jalal were as in love as ever. I would watch them as they looked into each other's eyes and held their gaze. I remember thinking how interesting it was to watch them have a whole discussion in this way without saying one word. I grew up believing that was what love looked like.

I am grateful that I met the versions of Shoukou and Jalal that I did. For me, Mamanee served as an inspiration to find my sense of self-worth inside of myself and not from the validation of others. Through her actions, she showed me to seek infinite respect and love from a partner in exchange for unending compassion and devotion. I also learned that as my perspective grows, so does my reality, so being curious about learning other perspectives serves me better than trying to prove my perspective is better or more right. To be honest, my ego gets in the way of this more often than I would like. I find so many of these lessons have to be relearned. It is not too different from becoming a master seamstress; it takes focus, practice, and continuous learning.

Of course, as grandchildren, there is a higher likelihood that we get to interact with and learn from a wiser, more grounded version of our grandparents than our parents did. Not always, but often, age itself can serve as a mechanism to gain perspective on life, allowing us to let go of parts of ourselves that don't serve us and to fine-tune the parts that do. Mamanee was a strong woman who challenged the societal norms of her time and chose her life. She was an excellent grandmother, wife, and seamstress. But how was she as a mom? My mom was the second-youngest of her six children and the youngest daughter. Mom shares:

> I was raised by an ambitious and driven mother who inspired me from afar but didn't seem to have time for me. I knew she loved me by providing for me, but I don't remember being comforted by her embrace or any intentional form of attention. It felt like I did not exist in her world. My mother favored her boys over her girls, which was common at the time. The boys were showered with love and gifts, while the girls were mostly in the background. As the youngest girl, I learned to adapt by not asking for much. It was a good life lesson in lowering expectations and seeking only what I truly needed. On the other hand, I was extremely lucky to have a father who did not adhere to the social norms expected of him. He was a strong advocate and protector of his daughters, even if that meant he had to be tough on his boys to make sure his girls had a voice. So my mother spoiled the boys, while my father was a fierce ally for us girls. I look back on my childhood with much gratitude for having felt safe and protected by my father. As my mother and I aged, we found our way to each other, but I always wondered if our bond could have been greater if she had seen me and my sisters as a priority in her life the way she did for my brothers.

I believe that because of how my mom was raised, she made sure Tina and I always knew that we were loved through both her words and actions. I was held, kissed, protected, and believed. There were many things I wished were different about my childhood, but through all of that, I always knew I had mom in my corner no matter what. And that gave me a sense of safety that I think too many children in this world grow up without.

So let's talk about mom, or, as most who know her call her, Fereshteh. Growing up, Fereshteh lived in a household that valued reading, and she was no exception. Her favorite topics were philosophy and psychology. These books helped her understand that we change and evolve over the course of our lives. She deduced that behavioral patterns are created and influenced by what we hear, read, do, feel, and interact with. So she decided at a young age that as her body grew, she would make sure her mind grew as well. Fereshteh, a curious soul, at the time of my writing this book, is seventy-six years old and still learning new skills and growing every single day.

In college, Fereshteh made some great friends. The closest of them was Noori. After college, Noori got married and had her first child. At this point, Fereshteh had decided that she would break from this particular social expectation and never tie herself to another through marriage. She was happy on her own, with no intention to marry. She had a good job and bought herself a condo. She was enjoying life while she learned about the world and herself.

During the next decade, Fereshteh dated a bit and even fell in love with a friend of hers. He also loved her, but life pulled them in different directions. Then she met someone at work. He was handsome and charming. They dated for a couple of years, and during that time, she realized she enjoyed loving and being loved in this way, so when he proposed, she agreed, and they married. Right after they married, life became complicated. He shared that he is unable to contribute financially to their lives because he is responsible for taking care of his mother. A couple of years later, Fereshteh and her husband bought a house together, and he immediately moved his mom into this house without Fereshteh's knowledge. At this point, after two miscarriages, Fereshteh was seven months pregnant. She moved in with her sister for a few weeks, but given her circumstances, she decided to forgive him and try again. So, his mother lived in their house while they rented elsewhere. He would spend not only his money but also much of his free time with his mother. Fereshteh did not seem like a priority in his life. She thought about leaving him many times, but she was raised to believe that as we make decisions, we have to be prepared to see them through no matter what. Changing course would have been a sign of her giving up and not following through with a commitment she had made. When their son was born after a very long and painful delivery, he was unable to take his first breath. Fereshteh and her husband grieved their loss for a year, and then she got pregnant again. This was when I entered their lives, and less than three years later, Tina came along.

The backdrop to all of this was a revolution that toppled the monarchy in Iran. The success of this revolution was surprising and unusual since the country was experiencing relative prosperity at the time. The revolution brought with it massive change at a rapid speed as an authoritarian, totalitarian Islamic government took over and instituted Shia law. Some of these laws include the prohibition of music and dance or the requirement for women to cover every part of their body except for their face and palms of their hands to save men from sexual temptation. Additionally, women were now considered half of a human in the eyes of the law.

In my late teens, I witnessed a bank robbery. I waited for the police to arrive and gave them my witness statement. As I was walking away, I watched the officer crumble up my statement and shove it in his pocket. I turned around and asked him why he did that, and he said that because I was the only witness and only half a human so my statement did not count. I remember standing there in shock with no words to express how I was feeling and how crazy that sounded. I was old enough that this experience did not shape how I saw myself or valued myself as a person who happens to be born female. But I was certainly not the norm. I had lived in the U.S. and had a perspective that many people who have grown up in post-revolution Iran do not have. To what extent do they believe this law to be an accurate representation of a person's worth in accordance with their gender assigned at birth?

Shortly after the revolution, the war started between Iran and Iraq and brought with it more fear and chaos, which, as you know, led to Fereshteh and her husband moving to the United States with their two daughters. Her priority was making sure her daughters were safe as she navigated this new foreign world. She was mostly alone in her loneliness. She had a brother who lived a few hours away whom she saw once a year at best. Her parents would come visit for a few weeks every other year and she had made friends with another mom in the apartment complex. She didn't share much about her life with her friend or her brother. Her parents knew she was unhappy, but she had made her choice in marriage, she thought, so it was up to her to find the strength to carry on or make a change. Eventually, she decided that she didn't want to live this way and talked to her husband about making a plan for divorce. A couple of months later, her husband took her kids to see his mother and never came home.

He called her from the airport, pretending to be at his brother's house to tell her that he and the kids would stay the night and come home the next day. The next day, they did not come home. She called his sister and brother. No news. She started calling his friends, work, hospitals, and morgues to no avail. She looked for her phone book to call her own brother for help. She could not find it. Two days later, she received a call from his brother saying that her kids and their dad were in Iran and that there was a letter for her in the mailbox. The letter explained that he was no longer able to live that way and work as much as he did. He wanted to be able to take care of his mother and be with his kids, so his solution was to go to Iran, where they had a home—the same one they had bought together—and where his mother lived. He left a ticket for her and asked her to join if she would like.

The following weeks were spent moving out of the apartment and selling or gifting all of their belongings. She pushed herself physically, with very little food or sleep, as she carried the impossible mental weight of what had happened. When she got to Iran and saw her kids, she knew she had to focus on them. They could not adapt without her, and she had to give them all she had, even though she found herself running on empty. So, after thirteen years of marriage, she got a divorce and focused on her daughters until they started to find their footing. During that time, she reconnected with her friend Noori from college. Noori's youngest child was the same age as me, so we would spend some weekends at the pool, which gave Fereshteh and Noori time to reconnect and carry life together. This also provided the opportunity for Fereshteh, now in her mid-forties to learn how to swim, which had been a dream of hers since youth.

Fereshteh also took a coding class and found a job at a small startup. She quickly worked her way up and found herself managing a team. She then moved to a larger company, where she continued to grow her career. During this time, she gained the financial ability to buy a house and give me and Tina access to more than our basic needs. For example, during high school, I was able to go on ski trips with friends or sign up at the fancy private recreation center close to our house, where I was able to make friends and have a social life I enjoyed. She would take us on vacation to different parts of the country, and we would go to the theater and local markets and experience the food and culture of different regions of Iran.

Over the course of a decade, I watched my mom transition from a lonely housewife to a strong career woman and leader in the community. I watched her take care of her aging mom with compassion and patience, healing her relationship with her mom to some extent. I watched her learn how to do things she had an interest in simply because she wanted to and could. She learned how to write computer programs, swim, paint, and build websites. She made friends and grew her community. She took care of her mind and body and challenged herself to learn from her own story and that of others so that she could live limitlessly. I have learned a great many lessons from my mom; perhaps the most important one is to be fearless. As I understand it, being fearless is not as much about not having fears as it is about challenging oneself to push past our fears so we can thrive as we live life, as opposed to sitting in fear while life happens to us. I find it interesting that most of our worries and fears never come to fruition, and when they do, we can handle them. So why spend so much time worrying or being afraid?

I remember asking mom if she was afraid to live alone. She shared that her biggest fear in life is being dependent on someone else. She said living alone is a badge of honor for her because it means she is able to take care of herself and us without any financial dependency on a partner or parent. She told me about a friend of Aunt Shay who was in an abusive relationship but could not afford to separate from her husband and take care of her kids. She said that was her biggest fear. I didn't realize it at the time, but that is kind of what her life was like in the United States when I was little. She was married to a husband who prioritized his mother over his wife and children. She was alone and had no meaningful income to take care of herself and her kids. She was trapped in a way. Because of this, both my sister and I have grown up with the privilege of never even considering not having financial freedom. As long as we have existed, the path was learn skills, get a job, and build on top of that foundation from there.

As her kids grew up and moved back to the United States, Fereshteh found herself in a much stronger place in life. She had a community of friends and family who supported her as she did them. She switched from full-time work to consulting, which gave her the freedom to work on projects of her choosing, empowering young women to find their voice and power in a world that tries to shrink them. Fereshteh has spent her life teaching women around her to love themselves and strive for fulfillment in life. She is inspiring. She is limitless. She is fearless. SHE IS MOM!

Chapter 5: Connected

"What it means to live life, is to experience the moment that is passing through you, and the next one and then the next". By **Michael A. Singer from *The Untethered Soul* © 2023**

Reza, a sweet nine-year-old boy, lived in the city of Mashhad in the northeast of Iran, a couple of hours away from the then-Russian, now Turkmenistan border. His dad, who was thirty-nine at the time, was a well-traveled and well-educated Border Sheriff, fluent in six languages, among them Russian, French, and German. Reza's mother, at twenty-two years of age, managed the household and her four children with the help of housemaids, cooks, and nannies. When not in school, Reza would spend his days chasing their German Shepherds around their multi-acre land and laying in the sun eating freshly picked fruit from their garden. Reza would watch his mother's hair dance in the wind as she rode her horse. His younger sister, Lila, would run around and pick flowers and chase butterflies while her nanny chased after her. The newly born twins, Freddy and Franky, were often inside the house, either sleeping or being fed.

One day, Reza's dad came home with a fever, nausea, and body aches. Weeks went by, and he didn't seem to be getting any better. After several local doctors were unable to provide any relief or explanation for his condition, it was recommended that they transfer him to a hospital in Tehran, roughly 500 miles away. A few days after Reza and his family traveled to Tehran, Lila fell ill and was diagnosed with diphtheria. While Reza's dad and sister were in the hospital, Reza started to feel pain in his side, and after several days of ignoring the pain, he was also addmited to the hospital for an emergency appendectomy. The hospital bills were stacking up, so his mom dismissed the home staff and sold their house in Mashhad, along with their car and most of their valuable belongings. She kept one nanny to help take care of the twins and a driver to help her get around. Reza was sent home a few days after surgery and Lila a few days after him. While they were home resting, Franky, one of the twins, developed a sore on his arm. Despite the doctors efforts to diagnose and cure the child, the one-year-old died, followed by Reza's dad one month later.

As a Border Sheriff, after twenty years of service, Reza's dad would qualify for a pension to be given to his family in the event of his death. Unfortunately, he passed away a few months shy of this threshold, which left his young wife and children without any income and, after paying the hospital bills, with no money at all. Reza's grandparents, however, were affluent. On his dad's side, his grandfather was on the General Council of Foreign Affairs. He had countless lands and properties and enough money to fund an entire town. Unfortunately, his greed was the reason he and his son were not in communication. After his son's death, he saw no reason to help his grandchildren and instead recommended that the children be placed in an orphanage and for Reza's mother to remarry. On Reza's mother's side, his grandfather was also wealthy. He owned several pharmacies and lived a very comfortable life, with much more than one needs or can spend in a lifetime. He had provided the house Reza grew up in, along with most everything in it, down to each fancy rug, as part of his daughter's dowry upon her marriage. He had six children, three of whom were girls, and he felt strongly that by raising them until they were thirteen and paying a generous dowry upon their marriage, he had done his duty as a father, and there was no need or appetite for further help.

Reza's mom did not see a realistic way for them to afford to stay in Tehran, and she didn't want to remarry and risk having to send her kids to boarding school, which would have been likely in her situation, so they moved back to Mashhad. With the last of the money from their house, she rented a room with a leaky roof and no plumbing or electricity. For the next few years, she would sell knitted items and help neighbors with chores in exchange for food for herself and her children. She would cook food on the equivalent of a camping stove and do laundry in the basement, where there was a community water spicket. After school, Reza would run errands for neighbors in exchange for food or goods. In the winter, he would use a metal bar to break up the multi-inch ice buildup in the outdoor washhouse so he could help his mom rinse off clothes and sheets. There were many days when Reza and his mother would not eat so that there would be enough for Lila and Fredy to have at least one good meal. As Reza got older, life got a bit easier. In his teenage years, he was able to tutor younger kids and make enough to help in a more impactful way. During his senior year of high school, Reza got a job at the local social services office, and they were able to move into a slightly nicer apartment.

As high school came to an end, Reza reached out to friends and family to seek help in finding a job that would support his going to college. An old childhood friend of his dad shared that the department of power in was Tehran is hiring and that he is willing to take Reza under his wing. So Reza moved to Tehran along with Freddy and their mother. Lila, sixteen at the time, was married off to a 30-year-old man and stayed in Mashhad with her husband. At the department of power, Reza started in the data warehouse, which back then was basically a literal warehouse full of filing cabinets. There, he met a young lady named Sheila. They started dating, and before they knew it, they were married, and she moved in with Reza, Freddy, and their mother. Shortly after their wedding, Reza and Sheila both took the college exams. Reza was accepted to study statistics, but unfortunately, Sheila didn't pass, and this created a rift between them. Over the following few months, their marriage failed in large part due to Reza's close relationship with his mother and Sheila's desire to be more of a priority in his life. Reza and Sheila divorced around one year after getting married.

For the next few years, Reza's days consisted of working in the morning and going to university in the evening. By the time he obtained his bachelor's degree, he had helped his mother purchase a small piece of land and build a home where she could live comfortably in Tehran. During this time, Freddy had moved to the United States to study abroad. At the same time, the department of power in Tehran was in the process of switching from a paper filing system to an electronic one, and they needed people who knew how to use computers. So, they gave Reza a multi-year sabbatical in exchange for his commitment to obtain a Master's Degree in Computer Science. Reza decided to join Freddy in California and enrolled at the same University.

Upon arriving, Reza quickly realized that he could not afford the incremental Alternative Language Services (ALS) classes that were recommended for foreign students. He decided to drop out of the ALS classes and take fewer classes in general for the first couple of semesters until he ramped up in English. In between semesters, Reza, Freddy, and their close friend, Lance, would go on road trips up and down the west coast. Reza fell in love with the waterfalls of Oregon, the redwoods of California, and everything in between. They spent any free time they had camping, fishing, hiking, and swimming in the lakes and rivers of the Pacific Northwest. A few years later, when Reza completed the master's program, despite his desire to stay, he returned to Iran. The money he had left for his mom was running out, and she needed him.

So Reza returned to Tehran, back to the department of power, now as a computer scientist with a nice new paycheck and fancy title. Over the next decade, Iran went through a revolution, resulting in the establishment of a radical Muslim government. During this time, Reza met a fearless and independent woman who was fighting for women's rights and very much against the radical new ways. After two years of dating, they married and had a couple of children. Once the war started, Reza and his family moved to the United States, a country he loved so dearly, in hopes of giving their kids a better life.

Reza, or dad as I know him, is in many ways still that young man camping on the west coast. After the big surprise that resulted in my unexpected time in Iran, I got to meet a version of my dad, who had been buried under the weight of life. He was no longer the dad who was working long hours, six days a week, with off-the-chart blood work that put him at a dangerously high risk for a heart attack. Instead, he was a sweet and kind man, fully dedicated to sharing the best parts of life with his daughters. He was patient, kind, and full of wisdom, which he gladly shared with us. He would often remind us to pause so we don't forget to connect with and enjoy life, as opposed to getting lost in the hustle and bustle of it all. You could visibly see when he was deep in enjoyment and gratitude. I would watch him randomly stop what he was doing, close his eyes, and let music sway him around, often bringing tears to his eyes. When we would ask him what he was feeling, he would explain to me and Tina that some person somewhere felt something strongly enough to pour it into music. Then, they practiced it until it encompassed their genuine and complete expression. After that they went through the trouble of recording we got to listen to it here from the comfort of our homes. He would say, “When you listen to music, try to connect with the artist by feeling what they shared through their art.”

Music is only one example of Dad’s deep connection with the world. By the time Tina and I were in our teens, we decided when we wanted to be at mom's house vs dad's. At this point, we mostly spent weekdays with Mom and weekends with Dad. We would go on lots of early morning hikes with Dad, and we were often the first ones on the trail. According to Dad, this was the best time of day to hike because we could hear and experience the world around us waking up. We would listen to the birds as they started their day and feel the wind as it carried the crisp air into our bodies. We would listen to the sound of our shoes on the dirt, mud, or snow as we fed our eyes with the diversity of flora and fauna of all shapes, sizes, and colors. We would take note of what type of clouds are above or how the sky is as beautiful and vast as the ocean. When we would get to the top, we would soak up the view as we waited for the little restaurant hut to open. Then we would get a pot of freshly brewed tea, a loaf of hot steaming bread fresh out of the oven, and a couple of sunny-side-up eggs. We would sit outside, enjoying our breakfast with full hearts and calm minds. He would always draw our attention to what a calm mind and a full heart felt like. My sister and I would roll our eyes, too young and stubborn to understand how precious of a lesson this was and how many years we would spend later in life trying to find our way back to this feeling.

On the way down, I would notice people coming up the trail with their heads down, passing by, paying no attention to all of the magic around them. They seemed to only care about getting to the top, not realizing the journey itself offered just as much joy and beauty as the destination. Thirty years have passed since my first hikes with Dad. We still enjoy walking along the trails and pointing out the variety of mushrooms, dancing ferns, and vibrant moss. At eighty-three, Dad's eyes still light up when he hears a woodpecker. So much so that he quietly sneaks off the trail to find the bird and enjoy his beauty from a closer distance. I clearly see little nine-year-old Reza alive in him when we are among trees and water. Unfortunately, we still watch people woosh past us, speeding toward the destination, missing the countless gifts of the journey itself.

Music and outdoor adventures were not the only gifts in life that Dad taught us to enjoy. We would frequent local, and sometimes not so local, farmer markets. Dad taught us to listen to the watermelons as he tapped their bellies to find the right one. They tell you when they are ready, he would say. He was right! We would pick up honey from the mountains embedded in honeycombs. He would point out the different colors the honey had based on the flowers the bees had interacted with. He would ask us to close our eyes and see if we could smell the difference as we would try a few small samples of honey. He taught us that food is not just something to shove into our bodies. Food is to nourish, to be enjoyed, and to be appreciated.

Dad has a way of treating the things that provide a calm mind and full heart as sacred and scarce. It was as if these things could be gone at any moment, and if we don't pause and appreciate them, we will miss the joy. Fresh food, good music, plants and animals, healthy bodies, and, above all things, time with loved ones. He would remind us often that nothing is forever. He would talk about his time in the Pacific Northwest often, and the conversation often ended with something like

> You never know how long you will have clean air to breathe, safe water to drink, fresh food to enjoy, beautiful trees to visit, clean rivers to swim in, a healthy

> body to carry you around, and most importantly, the company of those you love. Nothing is permanent and all things end. Don't waste your time with your head down, running toward a goal. The magic is in the journey.

Ok, so how is someone this connected and wise—the same someone who ripped his kids away from their mom, their life and all they knew? To understand that, we need to talk a bit more about his mother, my grandma Agnes.

Agnes, the second of six children, grew up in a family that provided her with everything she needed in life—at least monetarily. Her mother was an angry woman lacking any form of love or compassion for her girls. Per the standards of the time, Agnes was married to a 30-year-old man at the age of thirteen. Her husband was an assertive man who enjoyed excessive drinking and gambling, among other things. He was the life of the party, and she was his trophy to be used and flaunted as he saw fit. He was abusive and enjoyed inflicting pain in all the ways he knew how. When he died, Agnes, at twenty-two years old, found herself drowning in grief from the loss of her baby, responsible for taking care of herself and three children with no education, marketable skills, or help from friends and family. Any help that was offered was conditional, the cost of which she was unwilling to pay.

Her children became her whole world, and her oldest, Reza, became her rock. It was the four of them against the world. She became cold and hard toward most, except for her children. She even taught them Zargari, which is an ancient language spoken in very few places in Iran. She had learned this language from her caretaker as a child, and she taught it to her own children so they could speak privately when in public. She had decided that they trusted no one and needed no one but each other. As she explained it, she sacrificed everything for her children. I remember her often saying that she was young and beautiful when her husband died and could have remarried but sacrificed her own happiness to spare her children the pain of living with a man who would not love them like his own or being sent to boarding school or an orphanage. While there may have been some truth to this statement, it can also be true that she was protecting herself from yet another man who would use and abuse her like the last one.

On the other side of this relationship was Reza. The man who prioritized the needs of his mother above all else at the sacrifice of two marriages and traumatizing his own children. He speaks of his mother as if it were his job to "save" her. I have heard my dad say countless times that his mom gave her life for him and his siblings, so he owed it to her to do all he could to care for her. This may seem like a reasonable act of compassion on the surface, but without any boundaries, we find ourselves with a series of extremely bad decisions with traumatic impacts on innocent bystanders like my dad's first wife, Sheila, my mom Fereshteh, Tina, and myself. Not to mention Dad himself. The heavily toxic codependent relationship between Dad and Grandma was obvious to anyone who was looking except for Dad and Grandma.

The first few years after the big surprise, I was able to see up close how different their relationship was compared to the one I had with my own parents or other relationships I had witnessed up to that point or read about. On weekdays, Grandma would wake up and get dressed. She would then come to the dining room and sit in her chair. This chair was hers, and no one was allowed to sit in it but her. She would then ask Tina or me to bring her the TV controller, with no regard for anyone else who may have been watching something. She would then proceed to change the channel to whatever she wanted to watch and, while doing so, yell across the house, “REZA JAN,” which means dear Reza in Farsi. Dad would come rushing into the room with a cup of tea. She would then look at the tea and grimace. She would look at him and shake her head. He would then apologize, take the tea back into the kitchen, and pour her a fresh cup. He would then bring her the cup of tea another one or two times until it was brewed to her satisfaction and the color and smell of the cup were just right. I would sometimes watch him take the same cup back and forth until she said it was to her liking.

He would then take her breakfast order and do his best to get it right on the first try. Tina and I would get ready for school, quickly eat, and leave to avoid witnessing this long, drawn-out, painful-to-watch event. After school, Tina and I would mostly spend time in our room. We would do our homework, listen to music, read, sing or talk. We would join dad and grandma in the dining room for dinner and watch this whole painful thing all over again as dad ran back and forth to make sure his mother had exactly what she wanted, how she wanted it.

Grandma had made it very clear that she did not like Tina and me. We were not boys like the children of her firstborn should have been, and we were outspoken and independent, much like our mom. Whenever she tried to manipulate us, we would tell her we were not her puppets and that she should back off of us as well as dad. Her and dad would often speak in Zargari, so Tina and I mostly retreated to our room. In our room, we would often talk about how we felt sorry for dad being trapped by his mother. He, of course, didn't see it that way, so even having a discussion about it with him was difficult. As we got older, it became easier to find the words to help him see another perspective. He had become more receptive to our thoughts because I think he realized we were old enough to choose to live with mom and that he may lose us entirely if he didn't.

Throughout the years, every time Dad found a modicum of happiness, he was pulled back into the reality of his mother's needs and her complete inability to live without him. So he went back to Iran after college even though he wanted to stay in California; he put his wife and kids second to his mother for years, and eventually, when his wife was threatening divorce, and he realized he might lose his kids, he had to choose. He could not be the son, the father, or the husband he wanted to be while enjoying living in his favorite place in the world. So he prioritized. He chose the two things that he was unable to compromise on: his mother first and his children second. He did love my mom, and he wanted to have a life with her, us, and his mother, ideally in the United States, but he also knew that his mother would never accept his wife, and his wife would never be okay with being second priority to her abusive mother-in-law.

In his own words:

> "I was working twelve to fifteen hours, six days a week. I barely slept and had no friends or outlets. My blood pressure was through the roof. When I did take time off, we would go on a road trip, and your mom and I would argue the whole time. Your mom didn't want my mother in our lives. My mom hated that. I hated that, too. My mother gave up everything for me. I needed to be able to take care of her and see her every day. Your mom wanted a divorce and was going to take you away from me. You two are my whole life. I snapped and did the only thing I could do: I took you to a place where I had a house, and I could get full custody. The thought of living without seeing you both every day was not something I

> could handle. I would get home after midnight and watch you both sleep while I wept for the time I was missing with you. I did what I thought was the best option so I could be present in your lives."

When Dad turned sixty years old, he realized he had spent the entirety of his life striving to make his mother happy, to no avail. As a result, he found himself alone and unhappy and decided, for the first time, that it was time to focus inward. So he left his mother the house, and he rented a place in a mountain town. He told her he needed time to be by himself and did not share his number or address with her. He would call in once a week to check in on her for a few minutes. He would often hang up on her because she tried to guilt him into coming back with no regard for the boundaries he had set with her.

During his time away, he spent a lot of time outdoors, walking the trails and tending the garden at home. When I would join him, he would share tales of his life, and we would laugh and cry together as we both healed through sharing our stories and carrying the pain and joy together. During that year, I met Reza, the boy, and understood a bit about what he had been through. I watched my dad learn the difference between love and dependence.

I saw clearly in him then what I understand now to be part of the human experience for us all. Our experiences create patterns of behavior, and we subconsciously use these patterns to react in situations when a similar situation triggers us. In this case, when Reza's dad passed away, his mom was told to remarry and separate from her kids. She chose to keep her kids close and shut out the world. So 40 years later, when Reza's wife talks about getting divorced, the thought of losing full access to his kids, aka the trigger, leads him to seemingly choose but perhaps more react than choose, to keep his kids close and shut out the world.

It is not until we remember that we are conscious that we have a chance to become mindful enough to really choose. We can observe our thoughts and feelings and still choose despite what our reactive patterns may be, but it takes awareness, practice, and intent. As long as we stay on autopilot, we are essentially foregoing our right to free will because we are not actually choosing. Once we become aware enough to choose, the healing begins. Only then can we let go of the shame, guilt, judgment, and fear that are blocking us from truly loving ourselves and each other?

I get asked often if I have forgiven my dad. The answer is YES. For much of my life, my dad has been my best friend. He has been a kind and loving father who has taught me countless valuable life lessons, and with the exception of a short period of time, he has always been a source of safety and trust for me. In addition, I now carry a perspective much wider than that of the nine-year-old girl you heard from in the first chapter. I also see the perspective of the wife left behind, as well as the mother, who believed she was steering her son in the right direction, and the boy, who didn't see a key destructive pattern in his life until he was sixty. I don't know what I would have done in his shoes, and I don't agree with his decision. But I do understand why he felt the way he did and I see why he reacted the way he did as I try to look through the lens through which he saw the world at the time. We tend to easily judge each other for our decisions, even the trigger-induced reactive ones, without seeking to understand the full story. It's easy to label a person or a decision as good or bad, but I often find our stories are more complicated than what a simple label can provide.

Part 2 - Quest

Chapter 6: The American Dream

"Each one of us has to ask ourselves, What do I really want? Do I really want to be number one? Or do I want to be happy? If you want success, you may sacrifice your happiness for it. You can become a victim of success, but you can never become a victim of happiness".
By **Thích Nhất Hạnh**

After receiving the letter from the U.S. Department of Immigration, Dad, Tina, and I flew to Naples, Italy, for our green card interviews. We got there a day early and explored Naples. It was my first time in what I considered the real world since the big surprise eleven years ago. We went down to the beach and laid in the sun, then we walked back to the hotel through a farmers market and, picked up food and drinks and bought a couple of cute clothing items from one of the small boutiques along the way. Somehow, the air filling my lungs felt lighter. Or maybe that was me with a little extra pep in my step. I didn't have to be covered up under a robe and headscarf. I was outside for the first time in years in a sleeveless top and capris. My hair was in a simple ponytail, and I could feel the loose strands flowing around, tickling my face and neck as the sun wrapped me in her arms and nourished me. It's been twenty-one years since that day, and every time I step outside of my house and feel the wind, rain or sun on my skin, I think how deeply sad it is that so many women around the world go their whole lives unable or unallowed to enjoy this feeling.

We ate our pizza slices on our walk back to the hotel. When we got back to the room, Dad rinsed off the apricots and cherries and set them on the table next to the drinks. Growing up, we always had alcohol in the house, but with the exception of Dad having an occasional beer here or there, the bottles were mostly just taking up space and collecting dust. We had them in case there was interest during larger friend or family gatherings, which was rarely the case. I grew up knowing I could have a drink if I wanted, and I had tried a sip or two of my parent's drinks a few times and found the taste gross and never really felt the draw to consume alcohol. So when Dad put the few beers he had purchased on the table and handed me one, I was surprised and intrigued. I was twenty-one and had never really thought about drinking alcohol as a thing to do. At that moment, it felt like an acknowledgement of my adulthood and soon-to-be freedom, so I gladly took the beer and said "Salamati", which means "to health" in Farsi.

I took a few sips and then went to the bathroom. I noticed I felt giggly, and my cheeks were warm. Then I sat down and thought how weird it was that I had never noticed before how good it felt to pee. I washed my hands, floated out of the bathroom, and jumped back on the bed. I let dad know that I felt floaty and warm, and maybe I ate something weird, but not to worry because it felt good. He did one of his deep belly laughs, where you can feel how amused he is from across the room. He told me that I was feeling the effects of the beer and that how I am feeling is generally why people drink. I had not connected the dots between my few sips of beer and how I was feeling. He added that small sips over a length of time, pairing it with water, and moderation around how often I partake is key to having a healthy relationship with alcohol. That all made sense, so I took a mental note. I took another sip of my beer, laid back in bed, and had the best nap of my life.

The next morning, we got dressed and went to the U.S. embassy. We completed the physical tests and the written exam. We had to complete several medical tests before coming to Italy in preparation, but some of the tests they wanted to perform in person. That was when I learned how painful a mammogram can be. The day after, we went back for the in-person interviews. We signed in and sat down. Eventually, our names were called, and we went up to the window. The man sitting behind the window introduced himself as Mike something. He was a tall and lean man with kind eyes, and he laughed a bit like Santa Claus. For the next hour or two, he asked us each question. He wanted to understand why we had returned to Iran and the circumstances surrounding my parents' divorce. He reviewed the documents we had provided and asked if we had any questions. At the end, he stamped and signed three pieces of paper, and he said that these would act as our temporary green cards until we entered the United States and were given permanent residency cards. He then looked at me and said, You, ma'am, have forty-five days from your birthday to enter the United States. My birthday was a couple of weeks away, giving me a two-month window to go to Iran, say goodbye to my friends and family, and finally come back home.

For the next couple of months, I was a mix of excitement and sadness. I was so incredibly thrilled that I would be coming home and finally starting my life. I also felt a potent ache from leaving Mom behind. I knew once I became a naturalized citizen, I would be able to apply for a green card for mom. But that would take years. There was a five-year wait for me to qualify to apply for citizenship and another few years for her application to go through the process. I wasn't sure how often I would be able to afford to come to visit or how vacation time worked in the U.S. Thinking too far out was overwhelming, so I tried to focus on the short term. The plan was that I would stay with my cousins for a few months until Dad and Tina joined.

Mom put on a face throughout this time. She would tell me that I was all grown up and that it was time for me to go fly on my own, that she had her job and her friends, and that my job was now to worry about myself and not her. She was being sincere, but she was also sad about us moving away. We discussed this years later. Additionally, I didn't realize it at the time, but my dad's relationship with his mom had impacted my own view of how my relationship with my parents should be. My parents had sacrificed so much for me and made sure I had the skills and knowledge to succeed in life. I didn't understand that meant they were just really good parents and that I could go focus on my own life now. Instead, I believed that now it was my turn to take care of them. My job was to make money and prioritize their needs. Maybe I did not prioritize them over my romantic relationships as dad had done, but keep them as a high priority in my life. This pattern that I had unknowingly adopted from my dad was not as potent in me as it was in him, but it existed in me and shaped my view of life as a daughter and sister.

As I packed and said my goodbyes, I thought a lot about my mom and how she must have been hiding her sadness. I knew she was now a different woman than the one who cried in the bathroom all those years ago, but I felt a lot of guilt for even wanting to leave. I also thought about my dad and sister, who would be joining me later that year, and I was determined to be able to provide for them by the time they joined. I thought of the inconvenience I would be to my cousins as I took up space in their house and the help that I would need from them as I learned about how things worked and got settled in. At no point did I pause long enough to check in with myself and think about what I was feeling and why I was feeling it. I made a checklist and worked my way down the list until I found myself saying goodbye and getting on a plane. It was just me now. Just me.

I landed in Chicago for a plane exchange, but because I had entered the U.S., I had to pick up my luggage, go through customs, finalize my entry paperwork, and then check in the bags again for my flight to Denver. The plane I came in on was delayed by an hour and a half. This meant my three-hour layover was now only an hour and a half, and there was a chance I would miss my next flight. I got off the plane, hoping I wouldn't have to run to the bathroom as I had been doing for the past several hours of the flight. I quickly realized I had no idea how to navigate an airport, and I was in too much of a fog of fear and guilt to notice the giant signs above my head. I decided to go to the bathroom and get it together. I washed my face, brushed my teeth, and changed into fresh clothes. I still felt pretty sick, at the time thinking it was from the airplane food, later wondering if it was stress-induced. I decided to ask a security officer for help. He walked me to baggage claim and told me to follow the signs to customs and to make sure I got in the correct lane.

As I waited for my bags, it sank in. I was grossly unprepared to take on this new life. I knew I was good at problem-solving and would figure it out, but I had not realized till that moment how hard it would be to find my way in this great big world. I finally understood why everyone kept telling me that I was brave for doing this. I wasn't brave at all; I just didn't understand what it was that I was signing up for and had not paused long enough to be afraid.

At customs, they went through my luggage and did another mini-interview before stamping my passport and letting me know I would receive my green card in the mail in a few weeks. I checked in my bags and made it to my plane, but just barely. When I boarded the plane to Denver, the last of three flights on this twenty-three-hour adventure, I passed out from exhaustion almost immediately after finding my seat. I laid my head on the window, and I woke up to a turbulent landing a couple of hours later. I decided that I didn't want to burden my cousins with how I was feeling, so I was mostly quiet on the car ride home, which seemed to be fine since one of my cousins had plenty of updates of her own to share, and the distraction was very welcome. When we got to their place, I showered, we ate, and then I slept for the next eighteen hours.

Over the next few weeks, one of my cousins helped me get my driver's license and buy an old used car so I could start the job hunt. I was able to get a job as a cashier at a local mom-and-pop grocery store. I worked long hours and saved up. By the time Dad and Tina came later that year, I had found a small apartment for us and picked up some basic items from dollar stores and garage sales. It took Dad and Tina a while to get settled in and find jobs. Tina and I had to wait to enroll at the state university. We could not afford the tuition without financial aid, and to qualify for aid, we would have had to have lived in the state for at least twelve months.

Life was very hard those first few years. I worked seventy hours a week and didn't make the time to take care of myself. I was an athlete who stopped working out. I lost my connection to food and would eat anything that was around, which often included fast food since it was quick and cheap. I gained eighty pounds in two years and completely lost touch with the version of me that would pause and enjoy life's gifts; instead, she was replaced with someone who had to reluctantly peel herself out of bed to go to work, so her dad and sister had less to worry about. I didn't resent them for it, and they both worked part-time to help, but I did very much see it as my responsibility to take care of them. I now realize this was no different from my dad working long hours and deprioritizing himself for us and his mom all those years ago. I understood why he was on the verge of a heart attack and why he ran. I had nowhere to run to, of course. Life in Iran was not a life I wanted, so I had to find my way.

After a year, Tina and I enrolled at the state university. I maintained my long working hours and adjusted my work schedule to accommodate school. After another year, I realized I wanted to make more than the minimum wage, so I got a job as a bank teller. Unfortunately, forty hours a week of work, even at the higher pay, did not cover the bills, so I took on a second job, working part-time at one of the stores in the mall. They could accommodate the hours I was available in between the bank and classes. It was a basic retail job, and they would make a game out of what we sold. These games came with nice bonus checks if you were among the top few, so I learned very quickly how to match what customers wanted to the value of what the store was offering. The customers were happy, the store managers were happy, and I was making more money. This allowed me to fly back to Iran and visit Mom. We talked every week, but it was not the same as feeling her hug and seeing her smile in person. I was so grateful for the short visit in between semesters.

Another year passed, and a former coworker of mine reached out to me with an opportunity. She had left her job at the mall and was now selling furniture. She told me about the commission pay structure, and the numbers seemed unbelievably high. She said that the job was full-time and that they would work around my school schedule. This meant I wouldn't have to work two jobs, and it sounded too good to be true. I had a little over a year left before graduation, and having more time and money would make life a lot easier. Despite my doubts, I went for it. They hired me on the spot in the interview, and I started a couple of weeks later. Many of my coworkers were experienced salesmen. I was a sponge, and they were happy to show me the ropes. They taught me how to listen to what customers are saying and ask the right questions to uncover what they both need and want. They taught me about the differences in quality, pricing, and styles of furniture. They taught me how to sell ethically. It's an art, they would say, to match needs and wants with products. They taught me that if I have to manipulate or beg my way into a sale, I'm doing it wrong. I later realized what important lessons these were and that not all salespeople sold in this way.

Under the guidance of these new friends, I quickly became a top-performing salesperson, and I was making more money than I knew what to do with. The school was going well, and Tina and I bought our first house together. I bought a brand new car. Nothing too fancy, just an economy car with a sizable monthly payment. I experienced for the first time what it felt like to spend my own money out of desire and not purely out of a place of need. I was so grateful to my friend for encouraging me to join her at this company and to my mentors, who taught me to sell. I was grateful for the free time to hike, camp, and reconnect with nature. I was grateful for the time to grocery shop and cook delicious, healthy meals. Life was good!

After a year at the furniture store, I realized I had developed an unhealthy relationship with money. Money ruled my life now, and it was all I thought about. I would plan out how I would spend my paychecks well in advance of earning them. I started having nightmares about losing money or being poor. I had not yet learned to save, so I had no safety net. This progressed over months, and I was barely sleeping, and when I was awake, the very thought of not having money would send me into a panic attack. I didn't like this version of me, so I took out a loan for my last semester of college and left my job. By the time I was graduating, I realized that while my peers were taking internships over the past year, I was busy chasing money. I was, however, presented with a couple of exciting internship opportunities during my last semester. The first one passed on me because I was not yet a U.S. citizen and would not pass the security clearance. The other I had to reluctantly reject because it was unpaid and my family was counting on me financially.

By the time I graduated with degrees in math and physics, I didn't know what to do with them. I had no idea what I wanted. I had spent all of my time working and studying without thinking about what was next. The timing was also unfortunate, as the economy turned, and Tina and I lost our house. Over the next year, I worked in retail and worked my way up the managerial chain. Then, an interesting opportunity presented itself again. It was a partially commission-based sales job. I was not considering commission roles unless I saw a way to pivot into a different role quickly. This role was at a small tech startup where I could learn about the world of business and build a career. This time, I planned ahead. I would pay bills, then divide the remainder of my paycheck into three equal parts. One part went into savings, one part was donated to a cause I felt passionate about, and the third part went into a fun fund so I could do with it as I pleased. Being in a sales role was a short-term plan for me. I paid attention to everything: how decisions were made, who made them, what skills were needed, what was valued, and where the most job security and upward mobility opportunities existed.

After a few months of being recognized as one of the top performers, I noticed the best salespeople had a lower chance for promotions into other roles, but the second-tier salespeople were good enough to be noticed but not good enough that the company would hold them back. So, I took my foot off the gas a bit when selling, and I started mentoring and coaching new hires who came onto the team. This was a mental challenge because the world of sales is competitive, and the ego feels easily bruised when you see others higher on the charts, knowing you can easily outsell them. I did a lot of journaling during this time, addressing how I felt and coaching myself to lower my ego and instead focus on my plan. The company was hiring at a rapid pace but also losing people quickly, so I planted a few seeds with the right people about a training coach concept. This would be a sales manager role for new hires. As they came out of the 10-day classroom training, they would be managed by a coach who had been in their shoes and could show them the ropes. After a few months of consistently selling effectively, they would move on to their long-term teams under a more permanent sales manager. One month after I planted this seed, the decision-makers had an excellent idea of creating a sales training coach role. Fortunately for me and a peer of mine, we were obvious fits for this new role, and I was able to pivot away from direct commission sales. Doing so came with a significant pay cut, but I wasn't thinking short-term, and this was an acceptable tradeoff. I had decided that I wanted the American dream. The title, the money, and the ability to influence decisions.

After a year as a coach, I was promoted to be a sales manager, where I was responsible for managing a more permanent team of sales professionals. I put in the effort to teach this team what I had learned over the years and put my analytical skills to work. I would provide them with lists of people to call, and I would use the available data to guide them on what questions to ask, what products to sell, and what features to highlight for each client type. As a result, my team quickly became a top-performing team, and I was offered a role as a business analyst to replicate the efficient model I had built for my team for all sales teams across our three offices. During this time, I traveled back and forth from office to office and trained managers and salespeople on these new reports and processes. During my travels, I would meet non-sales employees residing in other offices and learn about what they do and what they like or dislike about their jobs. This was a great way for me to learn more about the business and assess what path I would take in my own career. As part of this, I learned about interesting external training programs that would help provide me with marketable skills and attractive certifications.

Roughly a year after I had moved into the business analyst role, the company I worked for acquired a smaller company. By then, I had completed several training series. Being certified as a Salesforce administrator, project manager, and scrum master meant I was one of the few people at the company who could help with complex, multifaceted technical projects. At this time, I was promoted to chief of staff and had probably the most fun of my career in that role. I was able to meet and work with leaders and third-party contractors with skills far exceeding my own. I continued to soak up every bit of knowledge that was shared, either directly or indirectly, by those around me. I turned down several higher-paying positions at other companies because the rate at which I was learning and growing far exceeded the value of a few extra dollars. I was also working on projects that I enjoyed, focused on improving both the employee and customer experience. During this time, I learned how to do my job very well and was recognized as a valuable asset to the company on several occasions. I learned that my problem-solving skills and lifetime obsession with organization and efficiency were not flaws of my personality but rather strengths in building my career.

After a very rewarding year as chief of staff, the company was acquired by a larger competitor. As part of this, a large portion of the company was laid off. I was one of a handful of people from my company who knew about the acquisition and upcoming layoffs. This resulted in twenty-something sleepless nights and an abundance of stress, knowing that many of the people that I knew and cared for were going to lose their jobs. Fortunately, the company that had acquired us took a caring approach and provided generous severance packages, including assistance in resume building and interview preparation for those impacted. I have been privy to several rounds of layoffs since then, and this was the only time in my career that I witnessed affected employees thanking the company for the way in which the layoffs were conducted. I learned a lot about why it is necessary to make hard decisions and how to make them in the kindest way possible.

After the acquisition was complete, I was offered a position to build out a strategy and operations team for the new combined companies. This was a challenge for many reasons. An exciting challenge, but a challenge. I was building a team from scratch. This team would be doing work focused on the creation, implementation and continuous enhancement of training, processes and systems with the goal of improving the employee and customer experience. This team's work would be an extension of what I had been doing for the last couple of years. The gap was that I had never formally worked on an operations team, so I spent a good amount of time researching, reading, and seeking advice from peers and mentors that I had stayed in touch with over my career. I felt confident that I could do this well and that I would make mistakes to learn from along the way. Most of the really great advice and tips came from leaders that I had met years prior who had experience working with or for larger companies with established operations functions. They helped me identify and shape job descriptions aligned with the skills I needed on the team. As I started managing a growing team, they helped me coach and support my team through scenarios I had no prior experience with. And I definitely made mistakes and learned from them. Initially, I was not always the best advocate and support system for my team, but each miss was an opportunity to learn and humbly grow. Again, I realized the value of community in my life, this time a career network.

Speaking of community, by this time, I had been back in the U.S. for nine years, and my mom had completed her green card interview. I had not seen her in person for seven years, and my heart ached to see her. The day Tina and I picked her up from the airport and brought her home was one of the best days of my life. I felt whole again. We were all finally in the same city. Well, at least for a year. Eventually, I was offered a promotion at work that was conditional on my moving to Seattle. So again, I left Mom, Tina, and Dad behind, this time in Denver. Fortunately, my work schedule and income accommodated my visiting them every 2 or 3 months.

On top of visiting my family, I was traveling about once a month for work during these years. I was able to stay in the best hotels and go to some of the most incredible restaurants with fancy people who talked about fancy things. I started to realize more and more that the conversations I am having are becoming more surface-level. People would talk about work of course, and somewhat about their home life, thought nothing about their struggles or feelings. There did not seem to be any safety around sharing our real life experiences. I remember a co-worker losing their father, and you could visibly see how sad and distraught he was when he returned from a short bereavement leave. But we didn't talk about it. It was not considered appropriate workplace talk, so everyone including my grieving coworker, pretended it never happened. Then, another coworker lost a child, the same thing happened. Another was going through a divorce not peep at work about their struggles. We talked about sports endlessly and, kids school performances, and other superficial things, but nothing real.

As the world around us started to change, people started bringing discussions that were previously considered inappropriate into the workplace. We openly talked about the

Me Too movement, and then black lives matter, the trump presidency, and wars around the world. This was a welcome change because we were talking about real issues outside of how to make the company more money, but the nature of these discussions was again superficial. Regardless of which side of each argument folks resided, it felt like we were all parroting. We seemed to repeat what we heard or read from others "on our side." There was no room for widening our perspectives. We had to fit in one of the two boxes or not talk about these issues at all. This felt more fake than when we didn't talk about these issues in the first place. We were all playing roles in this weird movie, and no one was allowed to go off-script. I started to feel disconnected and numb.

I wasn't necessarily anxious or stressed, but I also wasn't happy or fulfilled. I just mostly felt indifferent. I started to wonder what it was all for. I did all the things I set out to do. I helped my parents and sister all individually buy homes. I had a cool house with a sizable mortgage and a nice car. I bought what I needed without worry and had enough left over for a yearly vacation to anywhere of my choosing. What more could one want? Why wasn't I happy? But also, what was next? People around me talked about their boats and vacation homes, so I guess that was the next step, but that didn't sound appealing to me at all. If financial comfort and the collection of material items, experiences, and titles didn't bring joy and fulfillment, what would?

I started to think maybe my job had become too repetitive and unchallenging. I loved what I did, but at this point, my team was strong and in their groove, and the company had transitioned out of the rapid growth phase to a more stable state. I needed a new challenge. I started to ask around the company to see if my skills would be useful elsewhere. After a couple of months of exploring opportunities and assessing options, I decided to take a sabbatical. The company offered a two-month, partially paid sabbatical leave after several years of employment. So I traveled to a few European countries, spent a few weeks camping around the Pacific Northwest, and took a quick trip to Hawaii with my sister and some friends. While I was in Hawaii, I received a call from a colleague about an interesting opportunity. The People Team, which consisted of Human Resources and Recruiting, needed an operations leader. The job was similar to what I had been doing but also different enough that I would have to stretch and grow. We scheduled the interviews, and by the time I returned from my trip, I was offered the job.

I spent the next 3 years leading various operational and analytical teams. I enjoyed working in this department. The people with whom I interacted showed their human side more. They expressed feelings and talked about their experiences, not only as employees but also in life. They cared about what they did and the people they did it with. They seemed to have genuine care for employees across the company and took a more compassionate and less fear-based approach to leadership. For the first time in my career, I was shown what great leadership can look like. We supported each other through the ups and downs of life. When one of us had something heavy to carry, we carried it together. When one of us had joy in our life, it was shared and celebrated widely. For the first time, I learned what a healthy community outside of the immediate family structure feels like. I also learned that a work environment can feel comfortable and supportive. I am so grateful for these years. These were formative years for me in shaping my view of "what good looks like" in the how to show up better as a leader. Eventually, the small startup with 100 employees that I had joined a decade ago became a seven-thousand-person company. I learned that as companies grow, roles that were once wide become narrow. With more people and more processes comes more specificity around what one can participate in or influence. Teams tend to work more in silos, which means less cross-collaboration and more decisions coming from the top. None of this is a bad thing, necessarily, but it was not what I enjoyed. I missed solving big problems as opposed to fine-tuning something that is already mostly working well. So, I decided it was time. After ten years and countless lessons learned, it was time for me to pause and reassess what was next.

Chapter 7: Sex, Pleasure and Relationships

to behold in love
is to be held in love;
to receive this gift
is to be what's gifted;
we do not fall in love
-we are lifted!

"Behold and held" by Patrick Merle Sellin, from *My Soul To Keep* © 2023

I have thought about Mica and our shared first kiss a lot over the years. But the way in which I have thought about this memory has changed. As a nine-year-old girl, I felt guilty for the obvious pain that I caused her with my reaction, not understanding what exactly it was that I did or didn't do that hurt her. I felt a deep sense of shame in myself for not feeling anything when we kissed. I should have tried harder to feel something, I thought. After I had my first crush, I thought back on all the nice little things Mica had said or done to help me see that she liked me. At the time of the kiss, I had no way of understanding this, of course, yet the shame stayed. As I grew older, I understood that not feeling anything when she kissed me or not knowing that she liked me was nothing to be ashamed of. So, the feeling of guilt then shifted to how direct and honest I was with my feedback.

Outside of the experience with Mica, I had several other life examples that taught me that it is not good to be completely direct and honest. People seemed to have expectations for how I should express or not express my thoughts and feelings. When I did share my full self, it was often met with reactions like laughter or anger. My logical deductions did not take the recipient's emotional responses into account. By paying attention to this over the years, I have learned to be quite genuinely empathetic, a skill I continue to work on. But earlier in life, it meant that to be able to make friends, or sometimes just to be able to coexist, I had to show only a small subset of myself that was considered acceptable by others. In addition, sometimes, I applied pressure on myself to pretend to think and feel things that I didn't really think and feel at all. All of this so I could try to fit in.

So it turns out this whole socializing thing is pretty complicated. Everyone around me seemed to have it all figured out, or at least that was my perspective. The same way a child thinks their parents should have it all figured out. It seemed like everyone around me was a perfect puzzle piece from the same puzzle, and somehow, I was the weird piece that landed in the wrong box. They all clicked nicely together, and it was beautiful. So, it became my job to pay attention to what people expected of me. I paid attention to what people were saying, how their facial expressions and breathing patterns changed, and what caused fluctuations in their tone or body language. I made a sort of game out of it to see if I could predict how people would react based on what they were experiencing before they verbalized their reaction. I got quite good at this game. It made life easier to be able to read people and understand what they felt or expected.

What I did not expect was that I also started noticing familiar reactions in others, like self-doubt and insecurity, shame, fear, anxiety or judgment. I would see it in the smallest fluctuations in their facial muscles, length of breath, or even where in their body the breathing originated from. I found all of this fascinating. I realized that I tend to have emotional responses to their emotional responses. When someone was sad, I would also feel sad, and I would listen to them and find the right time to make them laugh a bit to remind them what it feels like. When someone was hard on themselves, I would offer a kinder perspective to remind them they could widen and choose their perspective. When someone was judgmental, I was judgmental of them and their judgement. Sometimes, I was even angry at them, realizing judgement in others, triggers judgment in me.

The more I pretended to be what others expected of me, the more I felt that I fit in and the more exhausted and lonely I became. I was surrounded by people, people that I didn't really know, and they did not know me. If I'm being honest, I didn't really know me either. I couldn't tell anymore which thoughts and feelings were mine and which ones were borrowed or adopted. It took so much effort to genuinely become these other versions of myself. I didn't want to be fake or pretend; I just wanted to be one of everyone. I remember reading an article as a young adult about an actor who lost himself in the role and committed suicide, and I remember thinking how relatable it was to get lost in a role.

To become these new, more acceptable versions of myself, I had to set aside many of the lessons I had been taught earlier in life. Mom would ask us to think critically and choose; instead, I spent decades conditioning myself to conform. I did, however, keep parts of who I was before all of this. I've always been a rebel. I've always fought for those who can't. I've always tried not to intentionally harm anyone, though I have not always been kind, intentionally or otherwise. Over the years, I have had a handful of relationships with people to whom I showed my full, truest self, or at least the version of myself that felt the most real to me at those times.

When I was twelve, among the books Mamanee lent me was a book about a woman's life. It was fiction but written like a memoir. The story followed this young girl's inner thoughts and adventures all the way until she was in her eighties and passed away. I don't remember the book's name, but I remember a specific chapter very well. This chapter starts off with the girl walking down the trail by her home and sitting under one of the trees to read. A crush of hers walked up to her and interrupted her reading. He sat on the ground next to her, and they talked. During their conversation, he asked if he could kiss her, and she agreed, so they did. While they were kissing, he asked if he could pleasure her. She was confused and shared that she didn't know what he meant. He asked her if she would trust him to show her, and she agreed. He proceeded to move his hand in between her legs and pleasure her with his fingers. I was in my room, lying on my bed, when I was reading this, and something happened. I started shaking and felt an explosion of pleasure as I read what was happening to this girl. I was fully clothed and was grasping the book as if it would fly away if I let go. I had my first orgasm simply by reading words on a page, though I didn't know that was what it was.

A few months later, I was home sick from school, and while my dad left to pick up some groceries, I found his porn stash. It was a small box in his closet, which we were not allowed into. He had placed a small piece of light blue thread on the box, I imagine, as a way to know if Tina or I went exploring where we shouldn't have. I rewinded one of the VHS tapes and watched. It was not at all what I expected. There was no discussion, no consent, no pleasure. Just sex. The man in the video took off his clothes, grabbed the already-naked woman, and shoved his penis inside of her. He pounded her hard and fast, and her big boobs bounced around. She was making noises seemingly more for his pleasure than that of her own. This felt nothing like my experience with the book, and I even felt a little grossed out.

I rewinded the tape back to its original spot, put it back in the box with the others, put the small piece of thread on top as it was, and went back to my room, trying to understand what I had seen. I revisited that box a few more times over the next year in hopes that I would find something more pleasurable, but to no avail.

A few years later, I met Maryam. When Maryam looked at me with her big brown eyes, I would feel butterflies. But I was living in Iran, where being heterosexual was the only way to be. Anything outside of that was considered a sin punishable by death. There were laws in Iran that could be broken. For example, music is illegal. But if the cops show up at your house or pull you over for listening to music, you can give them what they refer to as "sweets," which is basically a bribe, to go away. Same with alcohol and your scarf slipping back on your head. But even flirting outside of marriage between a man and woman was considered an unforgivable sin, and extreme punishment was generally considered normal even by non-religious people who lived there aside from the extreme Muslim government. If a boy had sex outside of marriage, he could be forgiven because giving into temptation is part of his nature as they explained it. But if a girl even kissed a boy, she would be shunned and reported to the government for torture and likely death. Now, if the participants in these flirtatious acts were of the same gender, then game over. No acceptance. No wiggle room. No way around it. Death!

So, my crush on Maryam scared me. I could not say anything. I felt an immense amount of guilt for even feeling what I felt. I would force myself not to think about her when I caught myself daydreaming. I thought about cutting myself as a distraction, but we would go swimming with Mom and her friends on a regular basis, so that was not an option. I thought about hurting myself in other ways but could not find a way that made sense to me. I hated myself for liking her that way. One day, during recess, she said she wanted to show me something. She took my hand, and we sneaked into an empty classroom. The janitor saw us, and she told him that we had period cramps and were going to lie down. He got embarrassed and went in the other direction. When we got into the classroom and closed the door, she read me a poem. It was one that she had written. It was about a fearless foreigner who had opened her eyes to a world outside of her own. She talked about her love for this person. Not sisterly love but one of infatuation and attraction. She read me the poem, and I felt tears rushing down my face. My heart was pounding, and I wanted to throw up. What did this mean? She liked me too? What do I do now?

Maryam asked me if she could kiss me, and I wanted to run out of the classroom, but I didn't want to hurt her, so instead, I told her how I felt. I told her I had had a crush on her for months and that I couldn't stop myself from thinking about her. I told her that I would love to kiss her and that I was not the brave girl she described in her poem. Instead, I am afraid of it, of her, of myself. I told her I didn't want to die and that we should not like each other. She came closer to me, and I could not move, and I could not look away from her. She wrapped her arms around me and held me. She said that she understood and that she did not want to pressure me. She said that our feelings are normal and natural and we should not feel ashamed of them, but that she understands my fear and shares it. I remembered that Aunt May had shared something similar about her and her roommate. I realized Aunt May may have been like me and that maybe it's the world around me that is broken, not me. I stopped crying, and I kissed her.

Maryam and I spent as much time as we could get away with in that classroom. Sometimes, our friends would join us, and we would read or sing together as a way to minimize the risk of being caught. One day, as we were walking home from school, one of the older high school girls asked if she could join us. She shared that she had followed us and knew what was happening. She shared that she is the same as us and that if we ever need an alibi or witness to vouch for us, she would be happy to say that she was with us, helping us study. To my knowledge, outside of Maryam, myself, and this older girl, no one knew what we were up to until Maryam's death. When she took her life, she left three letters. One for her parents. One for her sister Zahra. And one for me. The letter addressed to me, was hidden in Zahra's room, and the instructions to find the letter were given to Zahra in her letter in code. A few days after Maryam's passing, someone knocked on the door. Dad answered and told me it was one of my friends. I sluggishly made my way to the door, completely surprised to see Zahra. She said, "I was not here; burn this.". She handed me the letter and disappeared.

I went to the bathroom and turned on the shower. I sat on the toilet and opened the letter as my entire body shook. It was the poem she wrote for me. At the bottom of the poem, she wrote:

> Live your life boldly, and don't accept limitations. Show up well for yourself and others. Shine bright. Your directness is your strength. Don't let life happen to you. You are in control. I love you. Keep going. I love you, my Targol.

Maryam and I were secret girlfriends for three years, and just like that, it was over; she was gone, and my heart was torn into millions of little pieces scattered around outside of my body. I reread her letter thousands of times over the next few months. I would wake up to it, sleep to it, carry it with me on my hikes, and recite it to the birds and flowers over and over again. I would cry into the tree's arms as they held me up. I would write letters to Maryam and throw them in the river. My grief and anger over her leaving me in that way slowly poured out through the words on the page and the tears on my face. On the anniversary of her passing, I burned the letter along with my journal as I sat by the river and said goodbye to her. Maryam has been a secret I have kept for twenty-seven years, and by sharing this here, I celebrate our love and the time we spent together. I miss her and carry her with me always. I still recite her letter to myself every time I think of her.

It would be two years after her death before I developed a crush again. I was now going to college, and for the first time in a decade, I was sitting in co-ed classrooms. I was outspoken and smart, and by this point, I was well-versed in the art of fitting in but standing out just enough. I would get asked to go to parties and hikes on a regular basis. There were several young men who stood out from the rest. They were smart and active in the feminist protest scene. One seemed to show more interest in men than women, so we quickly became great friends. We didn't talk about our secrets, but we saw each other in a way others didn't. One of the other guys asked me to go on a hike with him and his friends. I agreed, and I found myself charmed by him. Mo was the guy who would call his friends out for saying stupid, sexist shit. He was bold and confident and freely talked about his thoughts and feelings. He was open to hearing that of others and didn't seem judgmental but rather genuinely curious. He was also well-read and well-traveled. He came from an affluent family and was generous in sharing his abundance with others. I found his generosity toward those in need refreshing. So, after a few hikes, when he asked me if I would want to grab coffee with him, a tiny piece of my heart returned to my body and did a quick flutter, so I agreed.

Mo and I dated for over a year before I moved to the U.S. During that year, we spent a lot of time hiking and even more time in my mom's basement having sex. Again, premarital sex is super-duper illegal in Iran, so even a neighbor seeing him with me in public would have been a red flag, let alone his sneaking into the apartment complex my mom lived in and us quietly hanging out in my mom's basement. Mo was attentive and communicated well. He was experienced and knew what to do, but he would also check in often to assess what I needed or wanted. I felt safe and loved in his arms. It felt good to love someone again. We both knew that it was likely I would have to move away at some point, but we fell hard anyway. We would talk about him coming with me, and he even spoke to his parents and mine about marriage. We were young and didn't necessarily want to get married, but we didn't want to be apart, and I didn't want to be in Iran, so marriage seemed like a good solution.

When the time came for me to move, he proposed, and we got engaged. Our plan was for me to go find my footing, then come back so we could marry, and for him to join. We maintained a long-distance relationship for two years, chatting daily. During those years, we both changed a lot, so when I went back to see him, we felt different together. He had developed jealous patterns where he did not trust me to be away from him, wanting me to provide constant updates to him on where I was, who I was with, and what I was doing. It didn't feel healthy. He also decided that he wanted to stay in Iran and that I should move back so we could start our lives together. On the other hand, I had gained a lot of weight and developed physical insecurities. I had also started college and was taking care of my family. I had just started making money and was finding my groove. I had no intention to return to Iran, and I certainly did not want to be married to someone who didn't trust me or themselves. So I broke it off, and it broke my heart. I loved him, or at least the version of him and us that we were prior. But that version of us didn't exist anymore, and I was just starting my journey in this new world and was excited to move forward.

Over the next decade, I had many more relationships and a good amount of sex outside of relationships as I explored my desires and sexuality. I found out what kind of porn I like, what sexual positions feel best, what kinds of partners I enjoy, and, of course, what I don't enjoy. I found myself in relationships with no sex, no pleasure, or both. I also found myself in relationships with lots of sex, lots of pleasure, or both. Surprisingly, I also found myself in an abusive relationship. Prior to this, I wondered why people find themselves in toxic relationships and why they put up with it. I would say things like, I would never put myself in that situation. Finding myself in one, I realized it can happen to any of us. It creeps up on you. You develop an attraction, fall in love, compromise, and compromise until you find yourself in a situation where you don't feel safe, are being controlled, physically or mentally abused, or all of the above. By the time you realize it, you are tangled in this thing that is sometimes good and sometimes not, and you convince yourself that the good outweighs the bad until you realize that you deserve better. That we all do. There is a version of you that loves yourself enough to want better for yourself. Regardless of the trauma and patterns that lead us into these situations, the journey always seems to be about self-love.

After I pulled myself out of that relationship, he proceeded to show up at my work and my apartment. It was not until he sent me a selfie of himself with my sister in the background that I decided to get a restraining order. I realized at that moment that I didn't love myself as much as I loved my sister because he was no more of a threat to her than he was to me. That was a scary realization. I started to question why I didn't love myself in that way. Why was it okay for this to go on for so long? Why didn't it matter if he hurt me, but it would have been devastating if he hurt Tina?

After this, I took a year off from sex and relationships. I spent time journaling again and learning about myself. I went to therapy and obtained tools to work through the trauma of the abusive relationship. It took me many tries to find a therapist that I connected well with. The first couple pushed God and religion on me. That was not a fit for me after having lived in an extremely religious environment. Then I had a few therapists that either minimized my experiences or hit on me. Then I found a therapist that I really enjoyed working with for years. She was an Argentinian-American woman in her fifties, and she seemed to understand me and have useful tools to share with me to help me help myself. She was kind and supportive but also not afraid to sprinkle in a bit of tough love and even share a few personal stories of her own to help me see a perspective different from my own.

I wrote a lot during the following few years. I started by writing about what I had learned over the course of my life. I wrote about myself and how I showed up in my interactions and relationships. What did I like about myself, and what didn't I like? How did I feel in different situations and groups? Which versions of me felt authentic and brought me joy, and which versions of me felt exhausting to maintain? Who did I have in my life that I felt completely safe with? Did I feel completely safe with myself, and was I willing to look at my darkest parts and lovingly coach myself honestly?

Going through these questions and writing truthfully to myself helped me see parts of myself that I had been ignoring. I saw that I used sarcasm as a tool to hurt those around me. I used my directness as a way to judge sharply. I had developed skepticism and mistrust of the world, and I had built frustration around having superficial discussions with those around me. I was craving something real and meaningful but wasn't sure what that meant or how to find it. I remember her asking me if I would be open to a psychedelic therapy session at one point, sharing that she thought I would benefit from it. She explained a bit about what that entailed, but given that I hadn't even tried cannabis at this point in my life, I was not ready for it, so we moved on from the topic pretty quickly.

At this point, I had moved to Seattle temporarily for work, and I met Jane. She also worked in the corporate world and had recently moved from San Francisco to Seattle. She had left an abusive husband behind and brought her two young children with her. We became quick friends and, eventually, more than that. We would spend all of our free time together with her kids, going to museums, reading, cooking, and building things. We were a family, and I was happy. I never imagined myself wanting kids, but I loved her kids, and we all fit in well together. After two years of really great times and no real arguments or disagreements, Jane told me that she is moving back to San Francisco so the kids can be closer to their dad. She provided no explanation and was not open to a discussion beyond that. By the end of the week, they had left, and I was left behind with a giant hole in my heart. I realized that sometimes you don't get an explanation or closure. Sometimes, you are left with curiosity and hurt, and you have to find a way to love yourself out of that. Sometimes, the hard is extra hard.

Around this time, my therapist retired and moved to Argentina. My work assignment also ended, and I moved back to Denver a month after Jane and my breakup. It was good to be closer to family, and I felt I was given the tools to work through my problems more effectively now. I didn’t tell my parents about Jane, but I did let them know that I was queer, and to my surprise, they both responded well. Mom, in the moment, said that she was happy for me for living my life as freely as I wanted. Dad asked me if that meant I was a lesbian, and I explained the difference between lesbian and pansexual. He was mostly quiet after that. A while later, he called me to tell me that he loves me and accepts who I am. He explained that he grew up in a country where there was no acceptance of the LGBTQIA community and that he has been paying attention over the past few years to make sure he learns and understands better. He added that he is proud of me for being who I am and for telling him. I did not expect any of this so it was lovely to feel safe in this way around my parents. My sister didn't care at all and reminded me that she loved me no matter what. She was hurt that I didn't let her know years ago and was sad that I was alone in this for so long, but she understood and respected my process.

A few months after returning to Denver, I jumped on a dating app for the first time. I was still getting over Jane and wasn't looking for anything specific, but I was lonely and figured I would try it. I was on the app for eight days. During that week, I received a steady flow of hate messages for being what the app called Curvey. Additionally, I received an abundance of unsolicited dick pics. It was overwhelming, and I could feel my physical insecurities growing. The girls on the app seemed to be just as unkind and demeaning as the guys. I was surprised by that. I started talking to this guy on day five. He seemed nice, and we talked a bit about our lives and what we were looking for. We decided to grab lunch the next day. We met at the restaurant and ordered our food. Over the following thirty minutes, he talked nonstop. He told me that he had just been released from prison for blowing up his sister's house while cooking meth. I truly didn't judge him as I understood by this point in my life that people are not the product of any one given decision and that we are all trying to figure out life. But I also knew that he and I were on different paths in life, and I explained to him that I was looking for something different. He then said that he understood and proceeded to ask me if I wanted to have sex with him in his car. I did not. I paid for lunch and left. He seemed upset with my response and followed me outside, making a scene. I went home, had an edible, and shut out the world for twenty-four hours.

On the evening of day seven, I picked up my phone to find a backlog of notifications from the dating app. As I went through them, one stood out. This guy had a very sweet profile and had sent me a kind message asking if I would be open to grabbing a drink with him the next day. I let him know that I was deleting the app this evening and a bit about my experience the day prior. He said something to the effect of "no pressure; we don't have to, but you seem cool, and I would like to get to know you better." I decided to meet up with him the next day for a drink. One drink turned into dinner, and several drinks later, we were making out in my car. He was kind, goofy, and down-to-earth. He cared deeply about our planet and all of the life on it, especially the animals. His background was in environmental science and biology, and he worked for the U.S. Forest Service. He seemed to find me attractive physically and otherwise, as I found him to be. I went home, and he called me a few hours later to talk more. I was making some donation bags in my closet when he called. I laid in my closet and talked to him for hours. He had also just gotten out of a relationship a few months prior and was not looking for anything serious, so it felt like a low-pressure friendship was building between us.

Our friendship and attraction grew quickly. We flowed well together. We shared values and had common interests. Three months later, we moved in together and were engaged. Three months after that, we had a small, ten-person wedding in our house with our immediate family. Within a year of being married, I was asked to move to Seattle for work, and we moved. At this point, he had quit his job and was enrolled in a master's degree program. My income covered our living expenses, and there was an opportunity for him to follow his passion, so it worked well for us. Neither of us fit squarely in the gender roles society assigns to us, but we fit in well together, and each took on chores and projects we enjoyed.

After moving to Seattle, life became harder. My job was demanding, with long hours and high stress. My physical insecurities had grown to the point where I didn't feel comfortable doing even the things that I loved, like hiking. Additionally, I was so exhausted all the time from being these different versions of myself at work that I didn't want to leave the house unless I had to. He would push me to get out when I was not working, and I was easily annoyed and very uncooperative. One weekend, we agreed to go kayaking. It was a new experience for me, and I remember thinking over and over again for the days leading up to it how embarrassed I would be if I fell in the water.

I remembered a video a coworker had shared a few years ago where an overweight woman got in a kayak and flipped, and I remember the combustion of laughter by my coworkers around me. But I knew I had to push myself out of this mindset of fear and anxiety, so I went anyway. And I had the best time, and I didn't want to come home. We spent the day out on the water and saw seals and jellyfish. It was magical. I also realized that I had maintained a lot of my upper body strength from being a boxer in high school, so kayaking was really no biggy. We went kayaking with a group of friends, and I saw that I was stronger and had higher endurance than most of them. Some of my fears and insecurities subsided as a result of this. So kayaking became our thing. We bought a couple of kayaks and spent most of our free time on the water. We explored the lakes around us as well as the Salish Sea from various put-in spots.

We kayaked around Mercer Island for twelve hours straight and explored Deception Pass from underneath during the tide switch, which was a bad idea but tons of fun.

But our relationship was not all fun. At that point in our lives, neither of us loved ourselves, and that bled into our relationship in the way of assumptions. He would say something, and I would assume he meant it in a different way, driven by my insecurities, and vice versa. I was close and loving with my family, and he came from an abusive family structure and a series of abusive relationships, so he could not understand my love for my family or my love for him, and I could not understand his mistrust and anger. We enjoyed the fun times and struggled through the hard times for years, often thinking about or talking about divorce. This went on for about five years before we adopted our friend's dog. The pandemic had started, and they had just had their second child. Loki was an anxious rescue that they had raised since before he was a year old. Now five, he quickly became our child. We poured ourselves into the well-being of this lovely creature, and he returned our love tenfold. Through loving him, I learned to be a mom and a better partner. I learned that unconditional love is a kind of expectation-free love. It's an accepting and compassionate kind of love. A judgement free kind of love. So I started loving my partner Jason that way too, but not entirely. This lesson, like most others, takes practice. Jason was also able to see how his own anxiety and anger affected Loki. Our little pup served as a reflection of our feelings and how we showed up, so we both started to grow and change.

Six months after adopting Loki, I quit my job after ten years, and for the first time in my life, I found myself in a place of financial stability. Not forever, but enough for me to take six months off and reconnect with life. The three of us spent much of these months hiking trails and camping. We explored waterfalls and ran up and down beaches on the Oregon Coast. I got to experience the magic my dad had talked about relentlessly for all of those years. I was able to reconnect with nature, with food, and with my own body in a way that I had not done since I got on that plane from Iran to the U.S. eighteen years prior. As Jason and I took the time to heal through our past traumas and arrive at the newer versions of ourselves, we expected to find our way closer to each other, but this was not the case. We were both growing but learning different lessons and not spending enough time directly and vulnerably talking about what we each needed, or better yet, accepting ourselves and each other as we were. Instead, we continued to make assumptions and fumble over each other. It wouldn't be for another two years before our relationship would change.

Chapter 8: Drugs or Medicine?

imagine
you're out surfing
and some thought-wave of
self-judgement swells and
you start anxious-ing
but
instead of paddling it
you love it into nothing
with a levee of
awareness…
"I'm sorry, please forgive me,
thank you, I love you,"
everytime it rushes at you
like that- every single wave
absolutely innocenced
till you're just floating
on a glassy ocean
of aloha

"Ho'oponopono" by Patrick Merle Sellin, from *My Soul To Keep* © 2023

My relationship with alcohol has changed over the years. Each time I have a drink, I hear my dad's guidance in my head.

> Small sips over time.
> Pair it with water.
> Moderation around how often and how much.

After that beer with Dad in Italy, I didn't have another drink for two years. I was pretty busy with work and maintaining a long-distance relationship, and I had not put effort into making new friends. My coworkers would invite me to parties occasionally, and eventually, I agreed to go with them. A few of us drove together and hung out for a while. They were smoking weed and drinking. One of them tapped the keg and poured me a beer. I slowly worked my way through that beer over the next hour. I drank plenty of water and paced myself. By the time I was on my second beer, there were what felt like hundreds of people in the house. There were people everywhere, and there were long lines for the bathroom. Some were peeing outside in the yard, and the house felt stuffy with cigarette and cannabis smoke. Someone asked me to dance, but I needed to get some air, so I walked outside and noticed the moon was out and some stars were visible. Then I heard one of my co-workers shouting my name from inside the house. As soon as he found me, he demanded we go to the garage, where some people were bubble wrestling. I wasn't sure what that meant, but I followed him and squeezed into the crowd of people to find an inflatable pool in the middle of the garage, filled halfway with bubble bath foam. Inside were 3 very fit, mostly unclothed people taking turns wrestling each other. It looked like fun, and everyone around me was super engaged in this activity and cheering for the wrestlers.

As I stood there looking down at my half-drank, now warm second beer, I realized how I was feeling did not match how much I had been drinking. I felt spacey and discombobulated. I slowly crawled—yes, literally crawled—out of the moshpit-like garage. My friend followed me out to check in on me, and I told him how I was feeling. First, he laughed at me because, apparently, the garage was a hot box, and to his eyes, I was obviously stoned from the cannabis smoke in the room. Then he offered me a ride home, which I gladly accepted since I could barely walk straight at this point. I remember walking out of the house with him and him helping me down the 3 or 4 steps in front of the house. He asked me to stay there so he could pull the car up, to which I responded, “Dude, its snowing!!!”. It was in the middle of summer in Denver, and it was 100% not snowing. What I thought was snow was some of the foam that had made it out from under the garage door into the front yard. He decided he should not leave me there alone and instead gave me a piggyback ride to his car. I remember his shirt feeling soft and his hair smelling good. When we got to my place, he dropped me off at the door and left. I rolled into bed and passed out. The next day, I was a mixture of shame for losing control and intrigue from losing control. It felt good to let my hair down, both literally and figuratively.

At this point, weed was not legal in Colorado yet, and I had no desire to smoke, so alcohol became a playground of sorts for me. I wanted to meet these other versions of me that giggled, flirted, and danced. I felt wild on alcohol, and it felt good not to BE GOOD. So, for the next decade, I became the shot girl. I would buy round after round of shots for old and new friends as we went to bars, clubs, and shows. I made lots of friends and later lost several of them to drugs and alcohol. I drank once or twice a month, but when I drank, I drank to party. I drank to break the rules. I drank to lose myself and find myself at the same time. But with all of this fun came a lot of shame. The morning after the blackouts, I remembered bits and pieces of the night before. I remembered enough to know I was mean to some and overly friendly with others. At the time, I worked in sales, and many of the people around me partied way harder than I did, so I convinced myself that it was all good. I believed I was not as far gone as others around me, so that meant that it was okay for me to stay on this self-destructive path.

One of the reasons I accepted the short-term work assignment in Seattle was to force a routine change in my life, as recommended by my therapist. When I arrived in Seattle, I made friends with a neighbor who was on her way up the chain at another tech company, and she enjoyed an occasional glass of wine in social settings. She was very, very grown up. Very,.... adult. I thought being friends with her would help me find a different way of living that does not include ongoing news of a friend's death due to an overdose or drug or alcohol-related accident. The change in perspective was welcome. Drugs were not my jam, but I was surrounded by them by acquaintance. Through my work with my therapist, I realized that my relationship with alcohol was akin to cutting or starving myself. It was a distraction that helped me keep all the heavy stuff locked up so I could pretend to function.

As I used the tools my therapist had shared with me, I found a pattern that was not obvious to me before. I was deeply insecure and craved feeling seen, appreciated and validated. I tied my happiness to the perspective of others and how people saw me mattered. More than anything. After all, I had spent my whole life carefully curating versions of myself that would fit well into different settings. So this meant the people in these settings had to give me a badge of approval so I could feel like all the work was worth it. So I could feel like I was one of them, so I could feel like I had achieved something. Seeing this pattern show up again and again in my journal helped me become more aware of how it felt when I was triggered. This meant that, over time, I learned to identify it as it was happening, as opposed to after the fact while writing about it. Eventually, I started to detect it right as I felt the feeling, which gave me a chance to coach myself away from feeling that way. I would give myself the validation that I needed, as opposed to waiting for someone else to give it to me. This was a big lesson because it meant I had what I needed inside of me, and I did not have to chase it externally. It also meant I had the power to do something about the feelings and did not have to drown in them. It gave me the power to choose to treat myself better than I had before.

After I moved back to Denver, a new friend of mine invited me to her place. She had a small, chill gathering of stoners. I shared with her that I was interested in trying cannabis but that I had never smoked anything and would prefer not to consume it that way. She brought over a brownie and told me to eat only a quarter. I decided to only eat half of what she had recommended. A few of us sat on the couch and watched TV. I can't remember what we were watching, but I do remember being super thirsty and seeing my water bottle on the ground in front of me. I tried for several minutes to reach out my arm from the couch and grab it, but I seemed to have lost all motor function. I tried and tried, but the couch had swallowed me whole, and I could not move even a finger. I remember thinking that I was paralyzed, and that was horrible because I was so thirsty. Just in time, my friend arrived to check on me. She asked me how I was, and all I could muster was a smile, followed by sticking my tongue out repeatedly. She laughed and asked if I was thirsty. I blinked, so she held the water bottle to my mouth. She then asked me if I would enjoy a hug. I nodded and realized I was not paralyzed because my neck moved, and my fingers were wiggling now. Like those plants that get droopy when they are thirsty, and then you water them and they come to life. She held me for what felt like forever, and then her friends jumped on the couch, and I found myself in the middle of a delicious group hug. Life finally made sense. This is what life is all about, I thought. Feeling safe and loved.

This sounds like a small thing, but that moment changed my life. I felt years of stress just evaporate out of my body as I was filled with love. After so many years of feeling nothing and feeling numb, I was alive. I felt like none of the goals, plans or worries mattered. It felt like the moments on top of the mountain where Dad would draw my attention to what it feels like to have a calm mind and a full heart. A little bit of weed in a safe place, combined with the loving embrace of trusted friends, reminded me to enjoy the journey and be present in the magic and joy of life. A lesson my dad had taught me over and over again and that I had completely lost connection with during young adulthood.

After this experience, I seldom drank alcohol, and eventually, in my late thirties, I started to develop an allergy. Now, every time I have a drink, I break out in hives. But before my body decided for me, I had already reduced my consumption. That may sound like something that would be hard and challenging, as it is for many, but luckily for me, I did not find that to be the case. After the changes in my friend groups and social settings, I did not find alcohol or the desire to consume it to be part of my life. With the exception of once or twice a year at a work social event, I did not see a need for it. So you may be thinking, did she just replace alcohol with weed? I suppose that is true enough, but it is also worth expanding further. When drinking alcohol, parts of me would sharpen, and parts of me would dull. I was not in control of choosing; the alcohol was. When consuming cannabis, however, I would become introspective and be able to peel back layers, finding more and more of myself, reshaping my perspective and widening my reality. For me, taking an edible is not something I do so I can fit in or be the life of the party. I sometimes take a bite of an edible and then journal, meditate, paint, or jump on the treadmill. With alcohol, my body was in charge, and my mind took a back seat. With edibles, my mind takes center stage while my body goes on autopilot.

This allows me to be deeply introspective. I pay attention to recurring ruminating thoughts and feelings so I can identify patterns in my behavior and learn from my triggers. It allows me to let go of thoughts and feelings that no longer serve me and feel whole and present. But while I think weed has helped me, one of the downsides of weed is that it's hard to follow a thought and remember where you are going. So much of the lessons get lost in the spaceyness of the mind on cannabis. Weed also gives me power munchies and makes it hard to be mindful when interacting with food. I have also, at times, used it as a crutch to feel calm superficially, ignoring the work I had to do internally to find my inner peace. This is not an advertisement for or against weed. I am just sharing my experiences and opinions in their truest form, as I understand them today. The point is that how this plant medicine is used matters.

Over time, as I did some internal work to better understand my psyche and widen my perspective, I started to feel better. Well, feel more, I should say. Not all the feelings I felt were good, but at least I was not numb anymore. I would go through spurts of depression where I had to force myself to follow work and life routines. I would have periods of waking up in a cold sweat just to go right into a panic attack. There were also times when I would look around, and all I saw was beauty and joy. I was becoming aware enough to understand that my mood changes were tied to my fears, judgment, and shame. I had simply accepted that that's life—a mix of good and bad, sometimes more of one than the other. I learned to appreciate the moments of balance and try to find my way back to them as often as I could. However, I didn't quite know how.

This would go on for a few years until I received a call from a friend of mine. She had struggled with depression and suicidal ideation for most of her life. On that call, I heard her giggle for the first time, and I noticed her voice seemed different—lighter somehow and maybe a bit more carefree. I shared my observation with her, and she said that her boyfriend had procured some magic mushrooms and that she had tried them. I asked her about her experience, and she said that she cried for a few hours, then laughed for a few hours and that the next day she was dehydrated and exhausted, but also that the heavy was not so heavy and the light was a bit lighter. I also remember her saying that she felt more like herself. She didn't share much past that, but that was enough to peak my interest.

So, I started doing research. I started to look for information online. I quickly found several knowledgeable communities that pointed me toward the studies that were done in the 1960s and the ones that were currently being done by top universities. Then, I started reading books on the topic. I read over thirty books the first year, and to say my interest had grown to an obsession is a valid statement. The more I read, the more I understood how prevalent mushrooms and other plant medicines have been in human history. Despite much of the culture and knowledge being destroyed, I was able to find books on the history and use of these plants in many parts of the world. I was fascinated. In my books, articles, videos and community discussions, I found that these plants have helped us heal and grow our minds and improve our lives over the course of most of human history. Some cultures use plants to heal the relationship between one's body and mind. Others to provide and strengthen spiritual connection. Some used it to grieve and connect with lost loved ones.

As I consumed information on this topic, my critical mind was just that: critical. At the time, I was thirty-seven, an atheist who believed in only what science has proven to us. This also meant that if you asked me what happens when we die, I would say nothing. Not, I don't know, but a stern and confident NOTHING. I believed in trying to be good and do good. But I also carried a lot of expectations for the world and people, including myself, that led to judgment and shame. I remained skeptical and even avidly against the spiritual content I came across while becoming more and more intrigued by the science behind the effects on the mind and mental health. In the midst of my research, I found some psychedelic mushrooms and decided to try them for myself.

I had read a lot about good trips and bad trips. A bad trip was referred to as an experience on psychedelics that one didn't want. From what I gathered, this could occur for many reasons. It was often reported that mushrooms and alcohol were consumed together or that mushrooms were consumed in a recreational setting where the participant was at a concert or social gathering, and there was a key missing piece from the experience: a sense of safety. But even when the participant consumed the mushrooms in a safe setting, sometimes they would still report dark and heavy, unwanted experiences. This concerned me.

To prepare for a trip, I had read that it can be helpful to eat healthy foods for at least one week prior. Additionally, getting good rest and engaging in active movement like exercise, dancing, yoga, or walking were recommended to enhance the experience. Preparing correctly physically seemed to also have a positive effect on the psyche and mindset of the journier, just as much as intentional time spent directly with the psyche in the forms of journaling or meditation.

Plant medicines give you what you need, not what you want. So this means going into a journey with expectations sets one up for disappointment vs. going in with intent. The difference is that intent focuses more on what you are bringing to the experience as opposed to what you are hoping to receive from it. A simple example of this would be “I want to heal my relationship with my father,” which is an expectation vs. “I am open to revisiting my relationship with my father and being open to widening my perspective,” which speaks more to one's intent.

Creating a safe, nurturing environment free of distractions seemed to be additive to the experience. In my case, I created a comfortable space in my living room on the floor. I had a folding mattress that I laid down with several blankets and pillows on and around it. I had read that some people feel cold after consuming psychedelic mushrooms, so I wanted to be prepared. I had also read that being close to nature can be a beautiful way to experience connection to our planet, and since I was indoors, I surrounded myself with plants. I also put on a nature documentary on the TV in the room while I played a multi-hour playlist that included only instrumental music and nature sounds on a portable speaker.

Lastly, I wanted to make sure I had a sober safety buddy handy in case I needed help. His job was to periodically check in on me but not interact with me unless I asked for help. I also had a rattle right next to me that I could use to call him over from the other room if needed. I knew that even with all of this preparation, a bad trip was possible and that I would have to trust myself to navigate the experience if that happened. I was told by a friend to make sure that I did not resist the medicine. If it wanted to show me something, I should relinquish control and go with it. This was what I was most worried about. Giving up control is not exactly something I wanted to do or was comfortable doing. I wasn't even sure I knew how to give up control if it came down to it. If I loosened my grip, what would I be like? What would I do? Scary thought. The good news is the experience would only last six hours, so I kept telling myself

> You can do anything for six hours
> It will end
> Nothing is forever
> You can do this.

Now that I had prepared for this experience, I had to figure out how much to take. Psychedelic mushrooms are generally consumed in 4 different dose ranges. First was the microdose, which is a very small amount taken daily with some break days and weeks built in to account for tolerance buildup in the body. At this dose, no psychedelic effects are felt, but recent studies point to enhancements in focus, energy levels, and memory for all age groups, especially for folks over fifty-five years of age. Then there are the macrodoses. For simplicity, let's call them low, moderate and high doses. A low dose is about ten to twenty times larger than a microdose and has been recommended as a good starting point for new journeys. The moderate dose provides a deeper psychedelic experience and requires relinquishing more control. The high dose is for experienced travelers who seek to experience separation from their ego and sense of self as well as well as strengthening their spiritual connection.

Every journey is unique, and I have read many trip reports where the journeyer experienced ego death with a small dose and others who continue to seek profound life-changing experiences after having experienced several underwhelming high doses. These categories are generalized, and there are a variety of psychedelic mushrooms, all with varying potency levels. The mushrooms that I had found were a basic low-potency strain, and I decided to start with a low dose to start safely.

While mushrooms can take up to an hour to take effect, in my case, I started to feel the effects after 20 minutes. First, I felt butterflies in my stomach. Sort of like the first day of school, with nervousness and excitement mixed together. Then I had a bit of nausea, so I had a small piece of ginger, and it subsided quickly. A few minutes after the nauseous feelings, I felt a sense of euphoria take over my body. I could not remember what physical pain felt like. My body was heavy and comfortable as I sank into the mattress and snuggled under the blanket. Then I started to feel cold, so I added another blanket. I was very aware of my body, really appreciating how good it felt to rotate my ankles and wrists and how amazing it felt to stretch. But movement brought with it nausea, so I tried to be gentle in my movement and mostly still otherwise.

I was thinking about several things at the same time. I remember paying attention to how cool it was that I was thinking through several different thoughts simultaneously, like a computer. It was like my brain was optimized somehow. First, I replayed some of my old therapy sessions in my head. It was like I was there again in the room, but not as me at the time, but rather as I was at the time of this experience, sitting next to my younger self, watching the conversation between my past self and my therapist, and also having a new conversation with my past self as my current self. It was a little bit reliving the experience and a little bit recreating the experience. Like current me, was a witness to previous me's life, and I was able to show her compassion and help her out.

At one point, past me was sharing her story about how she gained weight, and I felt a deep sense of anger. I followed the anger, and it took me back to my early 20s. Now I was with my even younger self, who had just moved to the U.S. We were sitting alone in our car, shoving a second chicken sandwich into our mouths despite feeling full. Then I heard her talking to herself, and I remembered the discussion like I was her again in that body at that time

> Do you really need the second sandwich? Didn't you weigh yourself this morning?
>
> I went to the gym so I could afford these calories.

> I have eaten enough; I don't need this. I'm not hungry.
>
> It's so delicious. I was stuck in Iran for years without access to fast food. I deserve this, and I'm not going to waste it.
>
> You just went grocery shopping; you have so much healthy food at home. Why are you eating this?
>
> It's so yummy. I don't feel like cooking. It's just a sandwich. Shut up. Shut up. Shut up.

My anger melted into sadness and compassion for this young girl. She was alone, afraid and stressed, and food helped her feel better. She just wanted to feel better and didn't know a better way. She carried the pain of all her past selves and the hardships that they had endured with her. She had not gone to therapy yet. She had lost much, grieved and processed little. So I started talking to her.

> I don't hate you. It's not your fault. I got you. I am here. You are not alone. I got you. You are safe. You are loved. You are not alone.

We cried together, and both she and I realized how much anger and shame she felt and that I had held onto. As I took deep breaths, I felt her find peace as she integrated with me. She was no longer a separate entity; she was now part of me. I was now a bit more whole than before. There was no more anger or shame associated with this memory, just love. I had healed through a part of my past that I was unaware I had to heal from.

I was about halfway through the journey at this point, and I decided to go upstairs to take a shower. By then, I felt more in my body and was ready to move. As I approached the stairs, I decided to crawl up like I did when I was a child. Not because

I could not walk or run up the stairs but because I simply thought it would be fun, and I giggled all the way up as I did as a toddler. As I approached the bathroom, I remembered having been warned about looking into mirrors. I was told that mirrors can show you things that you do not want to see. You may see yourself without the filters of your ego, and that would be a terrifying experience. I was dubious about this advice, and there was a part of me that felt strong enough to face this challenge, given my recent triumph downstairs. So I walked into the bathroom and looked straight into the mirror.

At first glance, I felt scared because I thought I saw two people in the mirror instead of one. As I got closer to the mirror, I realized there were, in fact, two people, both somewhat faded and translucent. The first was me. I saw my nappy hair and stretch marks, and my face looked fat and sad. I felt completely gross. The second was this beautiful goddess-looking creature with flowing hair and happiness oozing out of her eyes. Her skin glowed, and she moved as if she were water. I stared at her for a while and realized she reminded me of someone. Kind of like my mom but different.

> Wait, is that me too?
> Yes
> Am I both of these people?
> Yes
>
> Why do I always see myself as this first one? Am I sad all the time? How do others see me?
>
> Does it matter how others see me? Maybe? No?
>
> Will others see me as they see me, regardless of how I see myself?
>
> Yes.

Well, then, it doesn't matter how others see me. They will see me based on their perspective, despite how I see myself.

It does not matter how others see me. Judge me. Think of me.

It does matter how I see myself because I get to choose. I don't have to hate how I look. I can actually love myself.

Is it really that simple?
Yes
Really?
Yes

Key takeaways from today:

1. I have some work to do to forgive past selves and show them compassion.

2. I am capable of loving myself, and this matters because my perspective shapes my reality.

3. Mushrooms are fun. I see why they call it a trip.

Shower time.

As I chose the glowing, confident version of me with the kind, smiley eyes, the other one faded away, lighter and lighter, until they were gone. I saw myself for the first time since childhood. I saw the girl smiling back at me with her eyes in the mirror. I saw my playfulness, my sensuality, the rebel in me, the warrior within and the compassionate wise one all in one in the eyes of my reflection looking back at me. This was the last time I looked in the mirror and felt any sense of physical insecurity. I have had a handful of milliseconds of insecurity that didn't even fester for a whole second because this experience is still so vivid and potent in my memory, now five years later.

After this first experience, it would be a few months before I would try mushrooms again. The experience was profound and pleasant, but that was just a low dose, and I knew I had a lot of work ahead. I also read that most of the work happens after the journey. This was accurate. I spent months journaling my thoughts, feelings, memories, and even dreams. I realized how I was showing up in my dreams had changed. I was no longer angry, ashamed or fearful. I was confident and kind. Paying attention to how I showed up in my dreams gave me insight into my subconscious mind and patterns. How many of those were carried with me in my waking hours, where I would mindlessly react instead of mindfully choosing how to act?

My journals filled with patterns and triggers, and I started to feel lighter and lighter every day. I had not had a panic attack since the experience, and my depressive states were few and far between. In my journals, I also documented other changes that I had noticed in myself. When I went on hikes, birds, dogs and horses would come up to me and look into my eyes as if they were communicating with me and saw the change in me. My interactions with people had also changed. Compassion and appreciation came easily, and judgment less so. I also started noticing details on leaves and curves on trees. I recognized trees on trails we would frequent, and I now noticed the change in seasons and how the flora and fauna around me transitioned with the temperature shifts. I felt more connected.

For my next journey, I took a high dose. I trusted myself to be able to handle whatever happened. One of the common things I had read about was that time works differently when you are under the influence of plant medicines. I had not experienced this during my first journey. The intention I wrote down before the start of this trip was to find my courage. To face my fear of walking away from a substantial and stable income and a job that I mostly liked in order to challenge myself and grow.

Within a few minutes of feeling the effects of the medicine, I looked at my hands. When I wiggled my fingers, it looked like I had way more than 5 fingers. I thought this was fascinating, so I stared at my hand from different angles and moved my fingers for a while. Then I looked down at my chest. I was wearing a sleeveless purple top, and I became infatuated with the purple color of the fabric. Then I dove in. It felt like my consciousness flew out of my body and dove down into the very molecules and then the atoms of the shirt. The further I went, the more I realized how connected and pattern-based everything was. It felt incredible to travel microscopically and explore in this way. It was similar to looking into a microscope but very 3D and very vibrant.

Then I remembered I was here to do work, so I reminded myself not to waste time having fun. In the weeks after this journey, I explored why I thought having fun would be a waste of time, and I challenged the validity of this conditioned thought. Later, I learned that the experience and the process of learning lessons in this space can actually be quite fun and enjoyable, but during this particular journey I believed I couldn't have fun while I was doing the work, so I redirected myself and came back up into my body, and I looked around the room. The plants were breathing. They were moving, kind of like dancing, up and down with each breath, like our chest does when we breathe. That was also fascinating, so I spent time with the plants in the room, talking to each one and apologizing to the plants with yellow tips on their leaves. I wanted to go check on all the plants around the house, but my body was very heavy. Jason had just come to check on me, and I didn't want to call him back up to help me, so instead I crawled toward the stairs and made it to the second step before I decided that was the perfect place to reside for a while. I laid on the stairs and looked out of the little square window, and I watched the blue sky with perfect cotton candy clouds like a painting. I thought about how clouds are made of the same water that is in our oceans, lakes, rivers, food and our own bodies. Even the mushrooms I had consumed were once made out of almost entirely water. I giggled about that for a while.

Then I started to see the air. Like in between my face and the window, there was substance, and that substance had geometric shapes, and when I made noise, the geometric shapes would move, carried by the vibrations or sound waves. I could see sound move air and I found that to be pretty cool. I had brought the speaker with me to my new home on the stairs. It was playing music, and I could fully feel the music. Like really feel it. The music, like the plants, was alive, and it moved me. Not my body, but me, my consciousness. I was flowing around with the sounds coming out of the speaker, and with that, I took off again. This time, instead of going micro into purple atoms, I went macro up into the blue sky and out into the universe. I took a mental note that the macropatterns are super similar to the micropatterns from earlier. Everything is connected, I thought over and over again.

At this point, a sense of fear took over.

> You read about this. If you feel fear during the journey, the medicine is trying to show you something. Go with it. It's not forever.
>
> But it feels like I'm losing myself. I don't know where my body is. Am I going crazy? What if I lose my mind?

I can't let go. If I let go, I die. My sister needs me. My parents need me. Jason needs me. Loki needs me. I can't die.

Did I stop breathing? I can't hear my heartbeat anymore. Did I die?

Trust the process; don't waste this. Trust yourself and the medicine. Nothing is forever. If this is your time, then you will die. If not, you come back. If you lose your mind, so be it.

Let go. Control does not serve you. Let go. You can do it!

Ok fine. Fuck. Fine. Let's do it!

As soon as I decided to let go, I blasted off into what I would imagine a wormhole would feel like. First, I went to a familiar place. I was on earth. I'm not sure what time it was, but humans existed. I was next to the pyramids in Egypt. Anywhere I thought about, I was there in an instant. I didn't like that; I wanted to enjoy the journey and not just the destination. So I imagined riding in a hot air balloon. And there I was, above the clouds, floating around in a hot air balloon, or maybe I was the air or the balloon itself. This felt like my dream as a child, where I would leave my body and stargaze on the roof. This time, I flowed through the clouds, feeling a light mist on what would be my face if I had a body. Then, I flew below the clouds. I saw landscapes similar to looking outside of an airplane window, except I could feel the wind in my face and my thoughts navigating me around trees and mountains as my elevation changed. I traveled around the world, laid on sandy beaches, and swam in warm lakes. I ran up mountain trails and talked to animals in rainforests. After years and years of traveling, I decided to come back to check on my body. Jason and Loki were approaching. I was not ready to come back fully, so I paused them like you would a TV show, and I took off again. This time, I traveled the universe and what felt like other dimensions. Other life in other places.

After what felt like centuries of exploration, I returned to my body, and I unpaused Jason and Loki. They walked up to me, and Loki laid on top of me while Jason asked me if I was okay and why I was on the stairs. I told him I would explain later and that I was fine but needed more time. I then giggled at my use of the word time, having felt just a moment ago how abstract time truly is. He kissed my forehead and walked away while I sat there thinking about how we are all a speck of dust on a speck of time and how funny it is that we take ourselves and our supposed problems so seriously. We spend so much time ruminating on the past and fearing the future that we miss the present. Life is not happening in the past or future; it is happening now, in any given moment, and the more of these moments we miss, the less life we live. This feels just as profoundly true now, several years later, as it did that day.

After this experience, I quit my job and took six months off. As I explained before, Jason, Loki, and I spent most of this time camping or backpacking. What I left out earlier is that during this time, I had 3 more journeys on moderate doses of mushrooms, and each time, I was able to relive parts of my past. I had not realized how much guilt and shame I held in my body and psyche from the stories of my past selves. I had to learn to let go of the shame I felt for how I reacted to Mica's kiss. Or for hiding my love for Maryam and such a large part of myself for so many years. I had to apologize to my sister and forgive myself for making out with a boy she had a crush on in college. I didn't even like the guy. But I did like the attention he gave me, and I made out with him in front of her. I didn't want to intentionally hurt Tina, but I did want to feel something, even if that something would undoubtedly result in shame for me and hurt for Tina.

During this time, I wrote many letters. Some to my past selves. Some to my friends and family. And some to people who were no longer in my life. Some of these letters were for me to be able to put words to how I felt, what I was remorseful for, grateful for, learning, and releasing. I kept most of the letters to myself, with the exception of a handful that I felt important to share verbally or otherwise with the recipients.

Some of these letters were to my nine-year-old self. She still existed inside of me, fractured and shameful for what she believed to be her part in the kidnapping. After all of those years of journaling and therapy, she was still hiding in a corner of my psyche, reminding me that I didn't deserve to be happy, to be taken care of, to be loved, or to be whole because of what we did all those years ago. This one took a lot of energy to work through. We would write to each other, and I would tell her about my life and perspective, and she would reply with her own stories and views. This went on for months. She was stuck and kept repeating herself, not listening to or believing my words. I could feel her shame, as it was my own, but she could not feel my compassion and was unable to receive it as genuinely and purely as it was given.

The next year, I went to my first Ayahuasca ceremony. A friend of mine connected me to a community of people who have dedicated their lives to helping those around them heal and grow. This temple was nestled in the mountains in a faraway land. My warm body felt alive as I submerged it in the cold river flowing through the property. I made friends with a deer that I met on the property during my walk. She sat down in front of me and put her head in my hands, as Loki does when he wants a jaw and neck rub. Being there felt like living in a fairy tale. I felt so thankful to be there, and I had not even interacted with the medicine yet.

The temple was a large room built from wood and stone with high ceilings and wall-to-wall windows. Upon arrival, I was instructed to choose my seat, which consisted of a meditation cushion of my choosing out of the several that were laid out in a large circle around the room. I chose a spot in between the window and the hallway to the bathroom. This brought me some comfort, knowing I am in a new space and it will be dark during the ceremony. After my dip in the water, I spent my first few hours walking around the land and laying under a tree reading. When the time came, I sat in my seat in the temple along with twenty or so other travelers. We had six guides to keep us safe and facilitate the ceremony.

The first night, I had a hard time. My first bad trip, if you will. I had only ever journeyed in the comfort and safety of my own home or camp. This time was different. I found myself feeling uncomfortable in an unfamiliar place with people I did not know. I was also journeying with medicine, that was new for me. So, I did exactly what my research had told me not to do. I resisted the medicine. A while after drinking the medicine, I purged, which is to say, I vomited in the bucket that was provided to me before the start of the ceremony. Ayahuasca is generally a medicine that is used after sundown for several nights in a row. Purging, especially on the first night, is common as the body and the medicine get to know each other. It is called purging because the idea is that the medicine helps you release and cleanse what does not belong in your body and mind. It's kind of like taking your car for an oil change but for your body and mind. Purging can come in the form of vomiting, diarrhea, yawning, or sweating.

When I threw up, for just one second, I was embarrassed to be the first to purge in that way, but then I told myself it was good. I got it out of the way, so someone else does not have to be the first. I had learned by this point that life is a game of perspectives, so I was well-equipped to shift my perspective to adapt.

Before I purged, as the nausea built up in my system, I was having visions of a friend of mine. Over the past year, as I had taken an honest look at my behavioral patterns with the intention of assessing and learning, I had surrounded myself with others on a similar path of growth. With these new friends, we gave each other feedback directly and freely and received it humbly and gratefully. This particular friend and I had been friends for a few years at this point, and she was still hiding behind a mask, and I did not feel safe taking mine off in front of her. I had tried to give her feedback a few times, and she had become defensive. She also very openly shared her judgment of others, which I also took part in. I did not like the version of me that I was around her, and I was not yet strong enough to be fully myself around her and show her a different way. So, I had started to pull away from the relationship at the time, blaming her in my head for all of it. What the medicine was trying to show me was my own judgement and the need for my attention to revisit my expectations for not just this friend but also for myself and others in my life.

I had been resisting thinking about her during this journey. As soon as I stopped resisting, I learned that the medicine was trying to show me my own judgment and not that of my friends. I purged and immediately fell into a euphoric stillness deeper than any I had experienced with meditation or breathwork. Complete calm took over as I listened to the music for the rest of the night. Each night, an optional second and third cup of medicine is offered, which I decided not to participate in that first night.

The second night, I felt more ready. I had met some really great people during the day and felt more comfortable in the space. I knew a bit more about what this experience can be like and spent a few hours meditating and journaling to prepare myself for night two. During the day, I found myself feeling lighter, happier and filled with an abundance of gratitude. I remember sending several long texts to friends and family members, telling them what I appreciate about them and how much better my life is because of them. I felt a deep calling to share the love.

When we sat down for night two, I was still a bit nervous but mostly feeling strong and ready. Very shortly after drinking my first cup, I expanded. I will do my best to explain what this means. I felt like a tree expanding such that I felt my roots wrap around the very core of our planet and my branches reach out to the infinite ends of the universe. I was both present in my body, in the room, listening to the music, AND could see past the walls and ceiling, past the atmosphere, past the galaxy, as far as I wanted. In this state, I had access to knowledge. I could ask questions, and the responses would arrive. Sometimes the response was “you are not ready”, sometimes it was “I will tell you now, but it wont make sense to your human brain later”, and sometimes the response was an answer that I would remember often about things that later came true. This state feels like unlimited compassion, wisdom, and power all at once. It feels like love. And in all of this, there is perfect stillness. One can exist separate from the breath while experiencing the full magic of each breath as a separate and equally powerful entity. The sound of one's heartbeat is an intense piece of art serving as proof of existence in this life. At the same time, there is a connection to an internal, limitless wisdom. It's like being in a multidimensional library or being the library itself.

During this experience, there was a moment where I felt nine-year-old me very present, so I started to converse with her:

Thirty-nine-year-old me: Welcome, my love!

Nine-year-old me: I never got to go to a slumber party

Thirty-nine-year-old me: We are here now. Join us!

Nine-year-old me kind of took over my body. She started moving around to the music, and I could feel her joy.

Thirty-nine-year-old me: Want to see something cool?

Nine-year-old me: Yes!!!

Thirty-nine-year-old me: Scan through your future. See who you have become at thirty-nine.

Nine-year-old me started crying from joy and said, I never could have imagined this.

Thirty-nine-year-old me: We turned out pretty good, right? The hard stuff made us resilient and strong.

Nine-year-old me: And full of love.

We were both quiet for a while as we listened to a beautiful song that one of the guides shared.

Nine-year-old me: Best slumber party ever!!!

Thirty-nine-year-old me: Yup!!!

Since that night, she has been ever-present in my life. Somehow integrated with me but also present as herself. I call her my inner child, or rather, my healed inner child. There are other younger versions of me present as well, but nine-year-old me is particularly potent. I hear her giggles and feel her joy as we explore the trails and play music with friends. She reminds me to get over myself and have fun. To stop and play and live in joy. She is a constant reminder to be compassionate to all the people, animals and plants I interact with, reminding me that each of them may have a hurt inner child inside of them. She is a reminder to share my strength and what I have learned so that other inner children may heal and spread joy. She reminds me to share the light and help carry the heavy. It has been one of the greatest joys of my life to meet this carefree, happy version of the little girl I did not get to be before but am able to be now. I helped her see her story from a different angle, and she is helping me live more fully.

Do I think I would have found my inner child and helped her heal so we can do life in this way without the help of plant medicines. Yes! I believe I would have arrived at this place, but perhaps much later in life. For me, plant medicines helped me relive memories and rewrite my story as I widened my perspective at an expedited pace. Similar to writing, painting, and singing, plant medicines have been worthy allies on this path of healing and growth. They have allowed me to notice and remove blocks of ego, trauma, and cultural or societal conditioning that had created rigid thinking patterns that needed to be revisited. They reminded me to think about my thoughts, feelings and actions and better understand myself. They reminded me that life is not happening to me, rather life is something I get to live as a conscious being. They reminded me of the infinite sea of compassion and wisdom that lives inside of me. Inside of all of us. So … could I have arrived at this place without them? Yes! But I am glad that I had their help, and the support of a knowledgeable community, and an abundance of books, studies, and videos to help me learn and grow.

Part 3 - Happily Ever After

Chapter 9: The Human Experience

My joy is like a spring so warm
It makes flowers bloom all over the earth
My pain is like a river of tears
So vast that it fills the four oceans
Please call me by my true names
So I can hear my cries and laughter at once
So I can see that my joy and pain are one
Please call me by my true names
So that I may wake up
And the doors of my heart
Will be left open

A song by **Andy Fischer Price** based on a poem by **Thích Nhất Hạnh**, from *Please Call Me By My True Names © 2004*

If you have made it this far in the book, you are mostly caught up with my history. From here, I am going to share what changes I made over the past few years that set me on the path to fulfillment and purpose. In this chapter, I will explore the key perspective shifts and foundational beliefs that helped me reshape my reality, and in the following chapter, I will discuss lifestyle changes that I have found both helpful and necessary in support of this new life.

Over the past few years, as I have become more fully my unmasked self, people I interact with have started to take off their masks, and the world around me is becoming more real and meaningful each day. As I get to know people and hear about their lives, it has been striking how common the human experience really is. We each have our own stories, and each one is unique to us and our perspective. But each of these stories seems to come with common struggles and triumphs, which makes the human experience a shared one among us all. As you read my story, while likely different from your own, how often did you take note of your own desire to fit in, your own reasons for feeling shame and guilt, or your judgement of others? How often have you lived your life struggling with anxiety, depression, or grief? Do you notice fear holding you back from making changes in areas of your life where you are unhappy or unsatisfied? Have you found your younger selves stuck in the past, waiting for you to release them from their burdens by creating a safe inner space so that they can feel accepted and loved?

My journey to learn to live better, started by adding a critical lens to my ego, that is, my mind's way of thinking about the self. In our society at large, from a young age, we are taught that we each matter more than the next person. Not always in words, this lesson is often embedded in our lifestyles. We tend to care for ourselves and our families more than we care for others who we label as strangers. We walk by unhoused folks sleeping in tents or on cardboard boxes in the streets, sometimes even with anger toward them for living on what we deem to be our streets, often tying their hardship to drops in our property values as if money matters to us more than the quality of lives outside of our own. We eat animals that have been raped, tortured and murdered on a regular basis without pause or question because that is the norm. We overconsume, even though our obsession with obtaining largely unnecessary objects and experiences is tied to the unsustainable depletion of the gifts of our beautiful planet. We do this mindlessly, often without regard for our own well-being or that of all life on earth.

We struggle our way through life, largely caring about not much outside of our own needs and wants and sometimes that of our family members or close friends. We read about wars and genocide around the world with sad faces and broken hearts, but we are seldom prepared to sacrifice any of our own comforts to help others. So, we have inherently built self-centeredness and greed into our societal norms. Of course, natural selection is part of our evolution, which in the modern world translates to having a bigger house than our peers, more shiny toys, the newest technology, body-altering surgeries, and many other ways to impress and attract each other. But we have also evolved with complex, sentient minds capable of choice. So why don't we show up compassionately as opposed to selfishly, knowing that the way we are showing up today is destructive and widely harmful?

We have rebranded jealousy as competition in most of the world now. We reinforce this through sports, education, work, and even in our friendships and relationships. We take pride in being competitive. In winning and being better than each other. The pride we feel is the heart's response to the mind's ego. Our blind acceptance and reinforcement of this belief that we are better than one another or that we should strive to be better than one another has catastrophic results. Over ten thousand years ago, when the first cities were built and the first laws were written about owning property, people, animals, and resources, we set in stone the path that we are close to the end of now, and it's okay. This is the story of humanity. All things end, including us, and it does not matter if the end is a few months away, years, decades, centuries, or millennia. All things end, and accepting this is part of the journey to freedom from suffering. I believe it is important to accept this fact and go through the stages of grief as we would in processing any other form of loss. Our hope that the human species prevails indefinitely is our ego's response to this end.

Earth's human population has doubled in my lifetime and quadrupled in my dad's time here. To accommodate this, we raise and kill over 80 billion land animals and endless tons of fish and sea life, depleting our planet of its ability to sustain life. We turn a blind eye to the tens of thousands of species on the brink of extinction, many of which are critical to our own survival. When we step outside of our timeline and get a wider view, we clearly see that the end has already happened; we just have not seen it yet in our particular part of the timeline. We can't change what is to come, but each of us can show up better while we are here.

When any of us believe that we are more important than others, than all of the other people who are not us, and all other plant and animal life that is not us, then all we can do when we see hardship in others is either ignore it or be sad about it and hope it gets fixed because we don't see it as our responsibility to help. For much of human history, these beliefs have been reinforced through religion and political propaganda so what was once an evolutionary need for survival has now become a destructive global norm. As long as we are focused on our own problems and our own lives, we remain disconnected, stressed and alone. We will continue to mindlessly consume and spread harm, directly or indirectly. As soon as we figure out that life is meant to be carried together, inclusive of sacrifices to our own comfort, so that the good in life can spread further, we realize we don't need all the things we are chasing. We don't need a large portion of what we consume in the way of food, material items, travel, experiences, or comfort. We don’t need external validation or rewards for simply striving to show up well in this world. The dopamine hit we get from our constant cravings, wants, and desires does not serve us. While seemingly satisfying for a split second, the joy from this type of gratification is short-lived, and the side effect is a type of addiction to the recurring WANTING.

Okay, so if we looked at all of this and decided it was not working and we needed to find a better way—a better framework for our thoughts—what would that be? I used to think the solution was to buy a piece of land away from society so I could build my own little, healthy community protected from toxic societal norms. If only I were not participating in society, life would be better. Who's life would be better? Back to ego, we go. That solution may work to an extent for a handful of us, but what about the rest of us who can't afford to or are otherwise unable to live out this kind of dream? I have found that regardless of where I live and who I interact with, the first and most critical part of breaking this cycle of ego-driven living is **awareness**. That is, to remember that we are aware and conscious and not the reactive biproduct of our hardships and experiences.

Earlier, you read some of my inner thoughts as I debated with myself back and forth in front of the mirror or on the stairs, attempting to face my fears. But who am "I"? Am "I" the thoughts? Am I the feelings behind the thoughts? Or am I the observer of the thoughts and feelings? No matter what your religious, spiritual, or scientific beliefs and understandings, isn't it true that we are all part of the universe? Energy is dispersed across the universe in the form of stars, galaxies, novas, and, in the case of our planet, life. So, we are a piece of the energy of the universe. That seems like a fair and safe assumption. So, if that is true, that could also mean that I am not this body. I am not these thoughts. I am not these feelings. Rather, I am the aware, conscious energy that is experiencing life through this body's senses, thoughts, and feelings. Michael A. Singer does a beautiful job explaining this in his book "The Untethered Soul".

Okay, so why is this important? If I am not the thoughts and feelings but rather their observer, that gives me a whole new level of control that I had relinquished prior. As the observer, I have the ability to choose. Awareness provides us with free will. This means that as I inspect my thoughts, I can question which ones are based on ego and greed versus compassion and wisdom. As my patterns lead to emotional triggers, instead of reacting in accordance with these patterns and triggers, I can stop, think, and decide how I want to show up in that moment. It takes practice, but the gift of **choice** is freedom from conditioning. It is our conditioning to function in a broken society that places us neatly in a lonely, unhappy little box. Instead, the ability to choose gives us the freedom to expand beyond who we are expected to be so we can instead show up better in this world. For example, we can choose to inspire love and acceptance. To share strength. To live lives rich with happiness as we serve each other and all life on Earth. Not because we have to, but simply because we can.

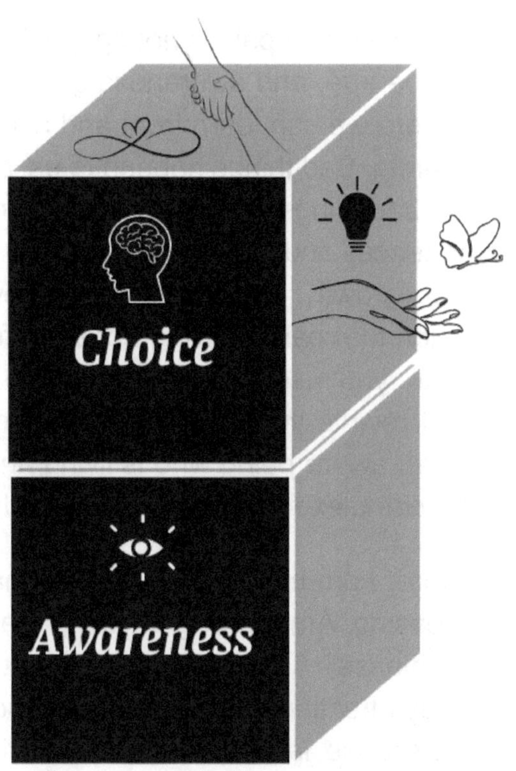

Being an aware observer also means we can decide what to hold onto and what to let go of. Another societal norm is holding on to pain and suffering. We ruminate on past experiences and hord the emotions they bring with them because we have been taught to do so and have not yet learned another way. Is it true that our past experiences are there to torture us as we relive painful moments in our minds? Or can it be that, as aware creatures, we are capable of paying attention to our memories, thoughts, and feelings so that we can learn from them and move forward? If I feel shame, I either had an expectation that was misplaced that I need to learn to let go of or I showed up poorly and need to learn to show up differently next time I am in a similar scenario. Playing the event over and over again and feeling shame without awareness to learn the lessons and release the shame, is simply suffering for no reason other than habit.

In Buddhism, it is said that pain is not optional, but suffering is. I believe this to be true, and awareness gives us the ability to live in a way where we can learn from and release things that lead to our suffering. Bad things happen to us, and we each do our fair share of bad things. But we don't have to be defined by our worst experiences and worst decisions. We can instead be defined by our growth and rebirth into new versions of ourselves through that pain, arriving not at suffering but at joy and peace. Can you use this framework to reshape your perspective and rewrite your own story? Is life happening to you or are you an aware being who is living and experiencing life through this complex sentient mind and body?

When I am aware, I am mindfully exploring what I am feeling, thinking, and sensing. Am I feeling anything that I should try to learn from and release? Are there thoughts that keep recurring that I need to pay attention to and perhaps choose differently? Are my shoulders tense, jaw clenched, or neck tight? Am I tired, bored, or overwhelmed? I started with a gentle singing bowl alarm on my phone that would go off every couple of hours during awake times to remind me to check in with myself. If I had the time, I would write down what I was experiencing during these times. If not, I would simply take five long, deep, intentional breaths and scan through my mind and body to see what I found. If I found something that needed my attention, I would simply ask myself why the thought or feeling was here and what I was meant to learn from it. If the lesson was obvious, I would take note and let the thoughts and feelings go. If the lesson was not obvious, I would still let the thoughts and feelings go, knowing I am not ready to see the lesson or that I am worrying and suffering needlessly. Over time, I found I was doing this organically more often than the alarm reminded me to do so, so I decided I didn't need the alarm. I also introduced this as a practice as I transitioned from one task to another. In between work meetings, during bio breaks or dog walks, while meditating, doing chores, sitting in traffic, or running errands. It was my little gift to myself. When I was busy and running from task to task, I would remind myself that I had time for five simple, deep breaths and that the sky would not fall if I took a minute to breathe. So I did, and it didn't. And the new healthy habit of awareness started to take form and make a home in my reality. The more of a habit this became, the less I suffered.

As the patterns of awareness and choice started to take shape, it became more and more obvious that I had been spending a lot of time on the past and future. Some of this time seemed to be spent in a healthy way. Revisiting parts of my past allowed me to heal, learn, and let go. Some of it, however, was not so healthy, and I would even go as far as calling it a waste of time. How much time was I spending, afraid of the unpredictability of the future or worried about things that mostly would not come to pass? How much time did I spend in the past ruminating on what I could not change, missing the lessons? Why was I doing this? Was everyone doing this? Largely, I found the answer to be yes. I believe this is one of those conditioned societal norms. It seemed to me that life does not have to be lived this way.

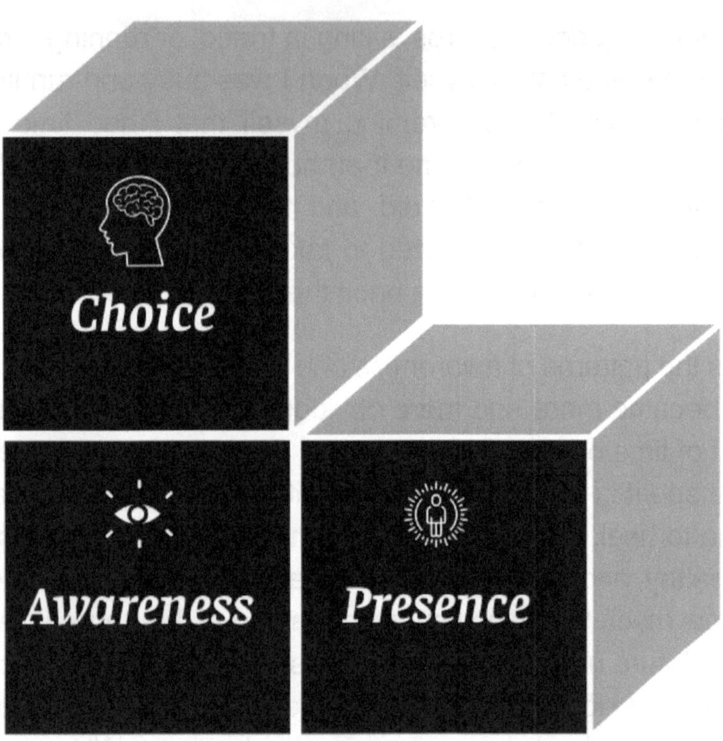

After all, life does not take place in the past or future; it's happening now. So my **presence** was needed so that I could experience and enjoy my life. As I started to pay attention to how often I was not present, I realized how much of life I was missing by fearing the future, ruminating on the past, or engaging in mindless activities that pulled me away from truly living. I started to track all screen time, even if it was reading a scientific article or watching an educational documentary. While some of it added value to my life, during these times, I was not fully present in my body, mind and environment. Then, I started noting how often I drove from point A to point B without remembering the drive. Where was I? Who was driving? How often was Loki asking me for cuddle time? What was I doing all day that was so important that it took the place of me being fully present and attentive to him? How often was I eating and not paying attention to whether I was hungry or full or how much I was eating? Was I tasting and smelling the food? Was I mindful of how much sleep or activity I was getting? Or was I just following routines or doing things out of habit without fully being present during any of them?

So, I followed the same process as I did with awareness. I set reminders and took time in between tasks to breathe. This time, instead of scanning my body and mind with the intention of visiting my thoughts and feelings, I scanned internally and externally with the simple intent to notice and understand what is happening in these moments. I watched the birds gather in our yard and form a line around our small garden. They would interact with each other while waiting for their turn, looking to my human eyes like they were catching up while running into each other. They would get quite flustered if one of them tried to squeeze in out of turn. I started noticing the clouds again. Was the big blue sky up there this whole time? Where was I? As I noticed I was hungry, I would think about all the lives that had touched my food before me. The bees that pollinated the flowers, the plants that turned the energy of the sun into healthy, nutritious yumminess, the farmers and growers of the food, the distributors, and the grocery store workers. I would spend time in awe of how many things had to go right for me to have a meal. I would smell and appreciate each ingredient as I chopped, sliced, and diced. It turns out that a byproduct of being present is **gratitude**. I would find myself overwhelmed with gratitude as my eyes swelled with tears and my heart exploded with love.

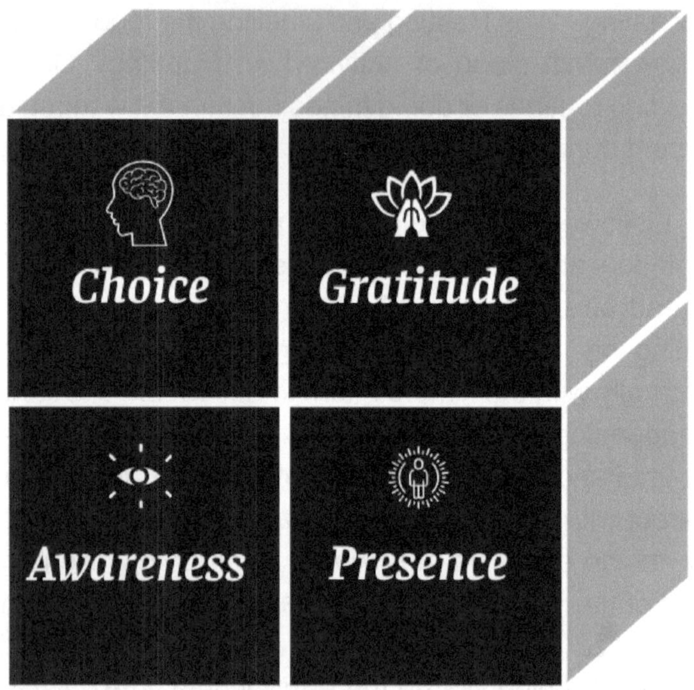

Like awareness and choice, presence and gratitude started to become more of a habit over time. Everything around me started to look like it was magic. Have you ever thought about how cool it is that we can see, smell, taste, touch and hear with these superpowers we call senses? Pausing long enough to pay attention meant I lived in the magic more often. I started to think about how trees experience life standing in the same spot from birth to death, all the while connected to each other underground, sharing nutrients and knowledge. Or how dogs see the world primarily through their noses and ears and how different this shared life must be for Loki and Bodhi in comparison to how I experience our life together. Everything became a source of wonder, and as I paid attention, I found lessons in how to live well all around me and in me. One of the biggest lessons has been compassion.

What do I mean when I say compassion? I mean love. But not just any love—unconditional love. Inclusive, all-encompassing love. Loving myself, yes, but also all other life, as if they are an extension of me and part of the same whole. An expectation-free, judgment-free, and shame-free kind of love. Accepting and forgiving. I have been learning to love in this way from Loki, my new puppy Bodhi, friends' children, and even my own healed inner child. What we call their innocence is the moral compass, isn't it? Children and animals that have had their basic needs met and have felt safe and loved since birth tend to act compassionately. As children, when our experience is not rooted in safety and love, we lose our instinctive ability to be fully compassionate. Even when children are raised in safety and love, we are still often taught through social norms to behave in uncompassionate, ego driven ways so that we can learn to function in a broken society.

So given this, how does one love in this way? To show up as a more compassionate version of myself, I had to start letting go of my expectations. I started paying attention to how many times a day I say or think things like "I should" or "they shouldn't.". Phrases like these were judgement and shame phrases. If I expect that I should or should not do something, that means I am not accepting myself as I am but rather expecting myself to be as I am not. Shame, shame, shame, until I learn to let go of the shame and break the behavioral pattern. Shame is there to remind me that I did not show up compassionately or that I had a conditioned expectation that was not met. So I learn, release and try again. The same is true with judgment, which comes from our expectations of others. Either way, who are these expectations serving?

What would happen if we shifted our perspective to understand that most of us are not aware most of the time, thus not choosing, instead, a reactive product of our conditioning? Years of experiences and interactions have led us to sometimes compassionate and sometimes non-compassionate reactions. Would this help us release some of the endless expectations that we have of ourselves and others?

Our minds consume data with every interaction from the second we are born. Every loving gaze. Every moment of fear. Every sensory response, every feeling, and the thoughts they result in. Every book we read, person we talk to, show we watch, and thing we eat is an input into our minds either directly or indirectly via the body's various signals. Our minds then use these inputs to be able to respond quickly as life happens. Much like artificial intelligence, our intelligence is built up from our experiences and inputs. So when experiences or inputs repeat themselves, a pattern is created, which leads to our reactions as similar scenarios arise. Each scenario is a trigger, sending us into autopilot to react accordingly. Inputs drive patterns. Patterns drive reactions. If we are reacting, that means we are not choosing to act with awareness. As we enter social groups, we consume similar content as others, on one or more topics. As a result, patterns are created and reinforced, all while dulling our sense of awareness and free will as our subconscious mind drives the vessel.

As we become more aware and inspire those around us to do the same, we are each presented with endless opportunities to choose how we show up in this life. And as I am given opportunities to choose, I hope to choose compassionately as often as I can. I have noticed that when I have not slept well or have too much going on, my temper runs short with Jason. This is not fair to him, of course, and it definitely is not a representation of me acting with choice. Rather, due to lack of sleep, I fall back into old habits where I react in mean and snippy ways. I have asked Jason to call me out when this happens so I can pay attention to it. Over time, I am getting better at recognizing it as it happens, leading to my sincere apology in the moment, and hopefully, in the long term, I will learn how to more consistently catch it before it happens so I can show up better for him as his partner. Being aware of this pattern in myself, while Jason has also become more aware of his unhealthy relationship patterns, combined with humility to hear and receive feedback from one another, has changed our relationship for the better. We have started to feel safe around each other to make mistakes, knowing we will be forgiven and loved as we are, as each of us sheds our expectations for ourselves and each other. The more we feel safe and loved, the more we show up compassionately in support of one another.

It is important to note that perfection is not the goal here. To be human is to be messy and to learn from it. So, there is never a version of me that is better than a version of you. I strive to be aware and present, and when I am, I try to sit in that as long as possible. I have found that as compassionate choices and expressions of gratitude have become more consistent new habits, life is not just more meaningful but also easier to live. I find myself less often flustered and more often at peace. My worries no longer consume me. My mistakes do not drown me in shame and my judgement of others is being replaced with understanding and a genuine curiosity to see things from new perspectives.

I have also stopped seeing the human journey and the lessons we learn as a linear path, implying that one person can be further along on their journey than another. I believe this way of thinking comes from a place of ego and feels too much like the competition trap. Instead, I like to imagine our human journey inside a sphere. This sphere is infinitely large with no boundaries, and it is full of an infinite number of lessons. In life, we grab as many of these lessons as we can. Some lessons we learn and hold onto. Some we lose and hopefully relearn.

Others we are not ready for. Every now and then, there is a lesson that we have learned and now understand more deeply, seeing it from a wider perspective. Its important to inspect the lessons we learn critically with awareness because sometimes we learn lessons that we have to unlearn later, realizing that lesson was birthed from unhealthy societal norms or our own ego, as opposed to being rooted in compassion and wisdom. To live is to learn, learn, and learn.

So in this perspective, all humans are experiencing life in the same infinite sphere with the same infinite lessons, but depending on our specific experiences and our place in space and time, we come across different lessons at different times. No one person is further along than another; we just accumulate different knowledge. By vulnerably sharing our experiences with each other, we open up the opportunity to learn. Not only can we learn from each other's perspectives, sharing opens the door to being challenged and humbled, or celebrated and lifted, as we all learn together and from each other. I may not realize a lesson I have recently learned is infact rooted in ego as opposed to compassion, but a friend may be able to shed light on that if I am creating a safe space for them to provide feedback. As a result, I can replace the lesson I learned with a new one that is more aligned with how I want to show up in this life.

We as humans share the human experience of living in this place in space and time, on earth in the twenty first century. We try to fit in with others, we adopt expectations that lead to shame or judgment. We spend much of our lives worrying about things that never happen and when they do, we figure them out, yet we continue to worry. We fear the uncontrollable and strive to control it despite knowing its a losing battle. We chase happiness and peace outside of ourselves and we continue to seek out new things to consume or experience to ease our pain and fill the whole we feel inside. As our world has become focused on efficiency and productivity, the sacrifice has been to our own well-being and quality of life. I think instinctively we all know this, whether we are willing to admit it or not. Deep down, I believe we all want to be happy and at peace, and we want our years here to matter in some way.

Over the past five years, as I have continued to broaden my perspective, it has led me here, and here is a fulfilling life full of happiness, inner peace and purpose. For the first time in my life, I fear nothing, feel everything, love in abundance, and feel connected to something profound. I am an aware being in a complex sentient body, that gets to live life in awe and wonder in each present moment. I choose to show up as compassionately and wisely as I can. When I can't, I am flawed and messy, which brings me joy because each messy human moment is a moment to learn from and grow through.

A very unexpected side effect of all of this has been the amount of strength it provides. I was conditioned to believe compassionate people are weak, but experience has taught me quite the opposite. I can say with genuine honesty that I am not afraid of anything and that I trust myself to be able to figure out life's challenges and show up well while doing it. I used to spend so much time thinking about what would happen if I lost my eyesight, got cancer or lost my job and house. What would happen if someone held a gun to my head or, worse, to the head of someone I loved? What if? What if? What if?

People around me would call me brave because I was not afraid to bungie jump or drive a race car. What I find funny about that is that we evolved with fear as a survival emotion. Fear is placed in us so we don't put ourselves in situations where we could die and so that we are motivated to find food, water and shelter. Now, we live in a world where we jump out of planes for fun and sit in our homes with packed refrigerators, heat, and plumbing. So, instead, our fear has run rampant in a direction that has made us sick. It has become an illness in us, and the only cure is to face the fears themselves. To let go of worries and to laugh in the face of silly fears that have no place in our aware and conscious minds. If I become blind, guess what? I will figure it out and be fine. If I get cancer and die from it, no worries; how we die is not of significance, but how we live is. So why not love our way through life? If someone holds a gun to a loved one's head, I believe that I am strong enough to forgive them and do all in my power to show them love and safety. I will dedicate intentional time to show them compassion as often as I am able to help them heal and grow through the hurt they carry. Lack of love and safety is what drives us to hate. To hurt. To react. I have created this love and safety for myself, and now I share it as wide and far as I can because, as a creature of choice, that is how I choose to show up. And when I get it wrong, I giggle at my human-ness and grow through it.

How we show up, once we are aware, matters. Not because we want to earn a pass through a gate after death or something or because we want to earn a gold star in this life. It is not about a reward. It cannot be in service of validating the ego because, as we have seen, that does not result in a fulfilled life. So, instead, we can show up well simply because we can. Simply because we are capable. I believe we need to overcome the need for constant validation and reward so that we can be authentically secure in ourselves and act with compassion because we are able. I have never in my life felt as free, as fearless and as connected as I do now.

Remember, its about the journey, not the destination. It's not about getting it right every time. There is no such thing as perfection and we are not born with expectations, we adopt them. Being aware and present means we can learn to genuinely live more and more fully each day. Its about figuring out, as aware beings, who we want to be in this world and how we want to influence the lives of those around us. Are you making the world around you better or is life happening to you? Are you taking the time to be patient and kind, or, like me, have you been telling yourself a story about how you are impatient because your mom is and its just who you are? Are you in a box made of conditioning, or are you a free creature of choice? Who are you, and how are you showing up? And most importantly, how are you showing up when things are hard? When you feel unsafe, when you feel angry, or when you feel scared. How are you showing up then?

> I am everyone, anyone, no one.
>
> I am everyone. We are all pieces of the energy of the universe. We are all connected.
>
> I am anyone. I am you, and you are me. I don’t matter more than you, nor you me.
>
> I am no one. I am a speck of dust on a speck of time, not defined by my ego and sense of self. I don't matter but how I show up does. How we as a collective show up matters.

Chapter 10: Path to Purpose

Creation is not all big bang
it is also like
the tardigrade-
small as grains of sand
curled into a ball
hibernating its miracle
waiting for a drop of water
to expand
in clumps of moss
content to be nothing for a while
without food, water, air-
do nothing but withstand
Himalayan snow, volcano
Space beyond
the Kármán line.
What more can it do
what more can we-
but dry husk the time
and then uncurl, begin
walking in the patient gait
of the slow and small?

"Water Bear" by Angela Sucich, from *Illuminated Creatures* © Finishing Line Press, 2023

In the last chapter, we talked about the perspective shifts that are foundational to living a fulfilling life. Here we will talk about lifestyle changes needed in support of this new path toward happiness, inner peace, and purpose.

Let's play pretend for a bit. Imagine yourself flowing around in an ocean. Don't worry about breathing underwater. Maybe you are a fish, or maybe it's just your consciousness flowing freely without the constraints of your body. Either way, you are moving, but you can't see where you are going because there are too many pieces of garbage in the water. You want to figure out where to go, but you find yourself mostly stuck in the same place, afraid to move into the unknown. Maybe eventually, you bravely flow in one direction or another in hopes of finding peaceful waters, but instead, you find more of the same.

Eventually, you decide you don't want to live this way and that it's time to clean up the water so you can enjoy the experience and move freely. This ocean is the ocean of life. And the rubbish that is obstructing us is the unhealthy habits and lifestyle norms that we have mindlessly adopted. If you were to remove these obstructions, you would find that this ocean is full of nutrients that feed you and serve life. As the water clears and we feel happiness and inner peace, the sunlight shines on densely nutritious areas. These areas are what we refer to as purpose. I have found that purpose is not one specific thing that each of us are meant to do; rather, much like the lessons in life, there are infinite ways in which we each can serve purpose during our lifetime. To see these paths clearly, we first need to clean our ocean, which we do by aligning our lifestyles to support us in the following areas: **Mind, Body, and Connection.**

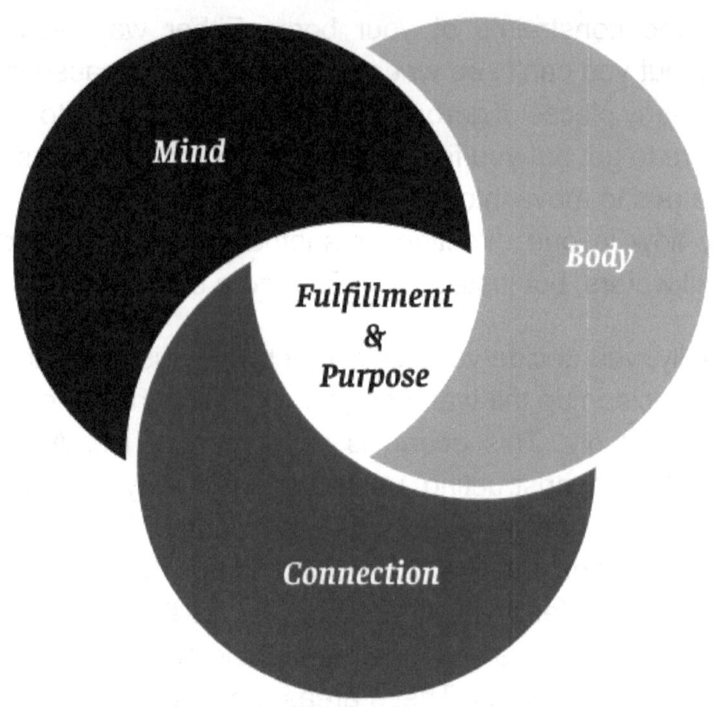

These three areas are largely overlapping and highly interconnected, which means positive lifestyle changes can impact one or more of these areas at one time. No area is more or less important than another. As we dive into each area, you may find you have healthy habits already formed in one or more areas. Again, the goal is not perfection, as perfection itself is a series of expectations that can lead to shame. Instead, I invite you to make a list of ideas for each area and choose **one or two things that you can do differently over a period of time** that make sense for you in support of your own path to happiness, inner peace, and purpose. Consider choosing one idea in support of an area you are already strong in and one in an area where you can challenge yourself to change or grow more. Building on your strengths is just as important as learning new skills and taking on too many changes at once can be overwhelming and discouraging. So start slow, celebrate the wins, and set the bar in a place where you can realistically meet it. And when you miss, celebrate that too and learn from it. Maybe you are stretching too far or too fast. Maybe you chose an area you are not yet ready to make a change in. That is also okay. Be kind to yourself and start small. There is no end goal here. There is no version of you that will ever be fully healed, fully fulfilled, or fully in peace one hundred percent of the time. We are humans and this is our life's journey. However short or long our life may be, we can spend the aware portion of that life to learn, grow and serve in any way we are able. Its never too late and we are all capable of rebirth and reinvention, if that is what we choose as aware beings. We will mess up and keep trying. There is no gold star to be chased here, just an intent and desire to show up well simply because we can, and to find joy and calm along the way.

Let's start with the area of the **mind** since we laid out the foundation in the last chapter. The mind is where our reality resides and our reality is made up of our perspective. We are not our thoughts or feelings. We are the observers. Aware, conscious subsets of the energy of the universe that are able to experience life through this body, in this place in space and time. We strive to be aware so that we can observe, learn from, and release our fears, shame, guilt, judgment, anxiety, etc. The more we can be present in our lives as opposed to fearing the future or ruminating on the past, the more we connect with the world around us, enjoy life's many gifts, and fearlessly choose how we show up. As we look into our past, we help our past selves heal and integrate with us by loving them, forgiving them, learning from them, and creating an internal environment where they can feel safe and accepted. We carry with us our healed inner children so they can remind us how to choose compassionately, feel deeply, have fun, and live in joy and wonder.

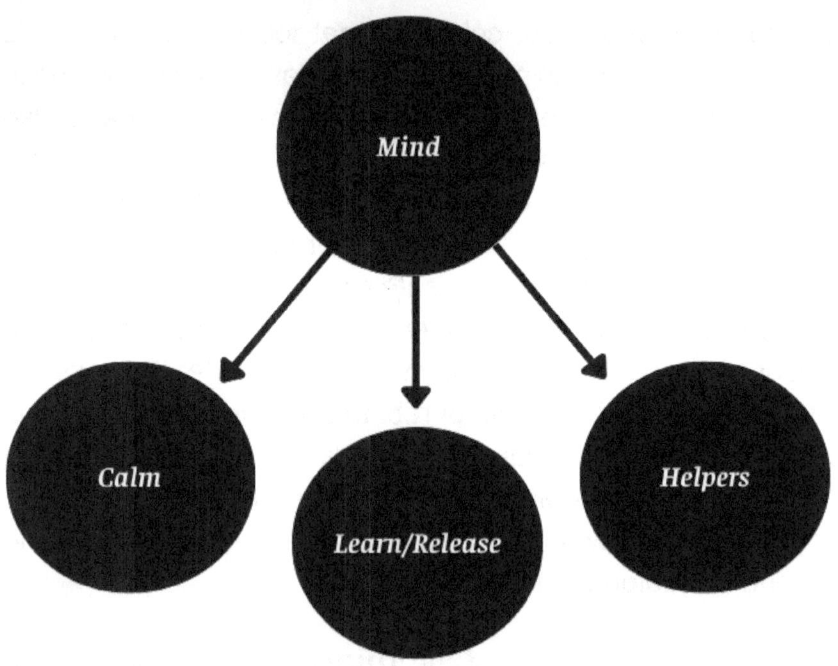

So what are some lifestyle habits we can adopt to support our minds in this introspective work? There are many practices that can help the mind heal, nurture, and strengthen. I will cover the three main practices that I have seen success with here: Calming the mind, learning and releasing, and partnering with helpers.

Let's start with **calming the mind**. For me, one of the most impactful practices I have adopted over the past decade has been meditation. There are many forms of meditation and breathwork. I started with a basic mindfulness practice. This consisted of me sitting in lotus pose for thirty minutes to an hour every day, observing thoughts and feelings that arose and setting them aside to train my mind to let go of worries and to find calm. The calmer my mind, the more aware and present I am, and the easier it is to let go of worries, fear, anxiety, or expectations leading to shame or judgement. And the more aware and present I am, the calmer my mind.

More recently, I have replaced some of my daily sit-down meditation practice with movement or flow meditation. This could mean I practice staying with my breath and setting aside thoughts and feelings while I do the dishes or something where my body is moving but does not need my full attention, allowing me to calm my mind. Or I dance to some music with my eyes closed, feeling what I hear and allowing my body to move as it wishes while I work on setting aside thoughts or feelings and calming my mind. Or more often for me, this means walking Loki and Bodhi on our favorite trail where I can be fully present with trees, slugs, ladybugs, bees, mushrooms, birds, and squirrels. During this time, instead of my thoughts and feelings, I pay attention to my senses. What I see, hear, smell, and feel as I touch the forest with my hands and feet. I notice the temperature change and how my skin feels as it does. I pay attention to the clouds, notifying me if there will be rain soon or I take note of the new growth slowly unwrapping itself from day to day. I listen to the birds warn each other as Loki or Bodhi get close to their trees and I watch the trees sway together as they dance in the wind.

The second practice is **learning and releasing**. Dedicating time to pay attention to my thoughts and feelings so that I can learn from them and release them has been a critical part of my journey. Journaling can be a great way to track progress and trends over time and its a practice that I have enjoyed participating in for most of my adult life. At times when I have not made the time to journal, I have instead utilized mood tracker apps or voice memos to myself to quickly track and work through something.

In addition to journaling about the mind's events, I shared in a previous chapter that I self-experimented with Psychadelic Mushrooms, Cannabis, and Ayahuasca and found them to be powerful guides and allies to learn from the past and release the corresponding thoughts and emotions. These medicines are not legal in many parts of the world. I am not promoting or encouraging the use of these plants and fungi. Rather, I am sharing my personal experiences and findings for informational purposes only. This book is intended for an adult audience and it is the responsibility of the reader or listener to adhere to local and national laws and regulations surrounding this topic and these substances. It is also important to consult with a medical practitioner in the event there is intent to consume. Many drugs and conditions can lead to unsafe and undesired interactions with some of these medicines.

The third practice in the area of the mind that I would like to cover here is **seeking help**. For me, this came both in the form of therapy and through conversations with trusted friends and family members. Talking to someone who creates a compassionate and safe space for me to talk through things out loud has been incredibly helpful. I have not always been good about asking for help, nor did I always have friends who I could fully feel comfortable being vulnerable with. Finding a good therapist was a beautiful turning point for me, followed by finding friends that took their masks off so that I could take off mine. I found no one has the answers to my problems, but allowing me to voice them and hearing perspectives outside of my own helped me find the answers to my problems with more ease.

What are some practices that you use in your life to calm your mind or learn from and release thoughts and feelings? Who in your life serves as a helper when you need a fresh perspective or a safe place to share your inner thoughts? Do you ask for help when you need or want it? Does your lifestyle include other mind-nurturing practices that we did not cover here?

As we know, the mind and **body** are quite related to one another. In support of the work we do to nurture and strengthen the mind and psyche, it is critical that we also take care of these vessels that we ride in during this life. The mind-body relationship is a bit of a chicken and egg situation because when we do a good job taking care of our bodies, our minds can process information more effectively. When we don't take care of our physical selves, the aware observer has a harder time focusing on the work of learning, releasing and calming the mind. On the other hand, the more we focus on our mental health, the better we feel in our bodies and the more energy we have to focus on the well-being of these sweet rides. And when we fail to do the introspective work in our minds, our bodies suffer in kind.

One recent example of this for me is post-hysterectomy. A few years ago, my doctor found some fibroids in my uterus. So we removed it, though we kept my ovaries so that I would not prematurely enter menopause. So I still have a hormonal cycle every month but no periods. Yay to no more periods! In my journals, I noticed that periodically, I experienced sadness or frustration with no obvious mental trigger. When pairing this with my cycle tracker app, I was surprised to find out that the sad or frustrated times largely coincided with the day before the start of my cycle. A fact that I had ignored most of my life was clearly outlined in my journals. Changes in my hormones effected my mood. Being aware of this enabled me to take extra good care of my body during these times. I made sure I ate and slept well, had enough activity, and spent time in nature. And the changes in mood became silly human moments that I would giggle at internally instead of sitting there pondering what had happened and what I was supposed to learn and release. Sometimes the body just needs to feel and the mind feels the feels in support of the body.

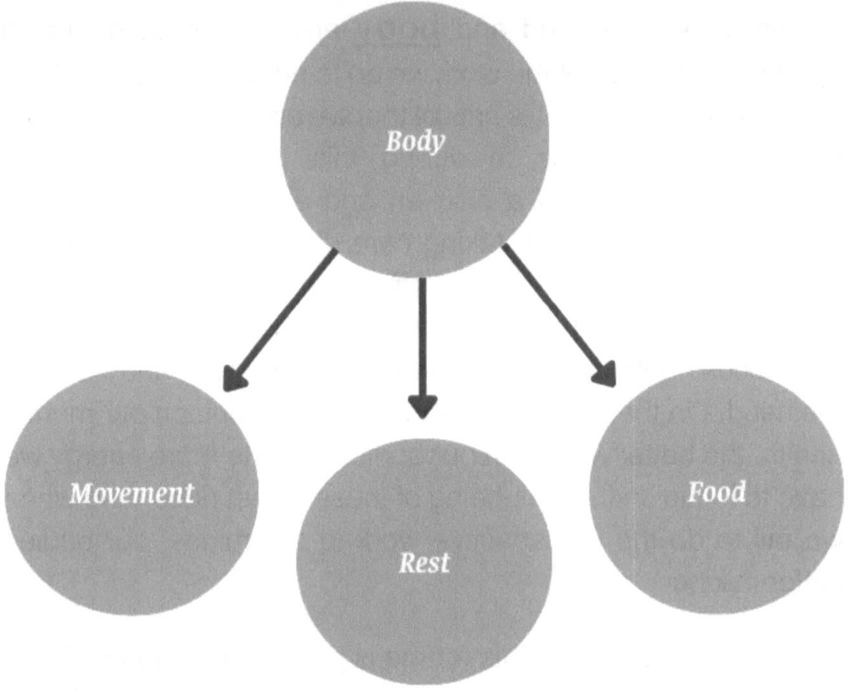

Like the mind, there are countless practices that activate health in the body. I will cover the three key practices of movement, rest and food here.

As I started making changes in my lifestyle to support both mind and body health, I had to constantly remind myself that the goal is not perfection. I found that the reminders I set on my phone to practice awareness and presence served as good check-ins with my body as well as my mind and I noticed that the two were not always aligned. For example, sometimes I felt lazy in my mind, but my body wanted to move or stretch. Sometimes, my mind was in a great mood and wanted to dance on the moon, but my body was exhausted and in need of rest. As I started to pay more attention to both my body and mind, I started to adjust my routines. I am learning that when I go to bed with the intention of working out in the morning because I want to instead of out of a sense of obligation, my morning is quite different. Rather than waking up to an unwanted alarm and hitting snooze endless times before reluctantly rolling out of bed, instead, I open my eyes and simply get up ready to move while feeling rested and energetic.

As I have aged, I have become more intentional about **movement**. I have been following a workout routine somewhat inconsistently for a few years. My routine has consisted of two days of cardio and three days of lifting each week. There would be days where I would do the activity reluctantly because I felt I had to. Other days, I loved doing the activity, and then there were the days that I would skip altogether. This routine felt too strict for me, so I started to reframe and add a bit of flexibility. I generally categorize the days into "help my heart feel alive" days and "help my muscles feel alive days". So now, when I wake up and it is a heart day, I know I can choose any activity that will increase my heart rate for a while. If I am not in the mood to jump on the treadmill, I go on a hilly hike or dance for an hour. I do what feels good, and my mind and body feel much more aligned. On muscle days, if I do not want to do squats and lunges in the gym, I put on my fifty-pound backpacking pack and go up and down the stairs in my house, hearing the little girl inside of me giggle at what Loki and Bodhi think of this as they follow me on this journey.

But even with these changes, my physical health tends to be one of the first things to take a back seat when life gets busy. The cycle of deprioritizing myself and feeling shame because of it has become a less consistent reaction over the past year, but it continues to be a pattern in my life. I celebrate where I am on this journey, and I have more work to do. I have learned that my body loves to move, and my mind is more aware and present when I do. And so the journey continues.

In addition to focusing on movement, I have increased my focus on resting. In my teens and early adulthood, I could sleep for 13 hours straight and feel rested when I woke. As I have aged and alarm clocks for work and scheduled appointments and dog care have entered my life, I have had to be more mindful of how much and the quality of rest I receive. I love to sleep but have not always been able to sleep well. During periods of high anxiety, fear, or depression, my ability to fall asleep and stay asleep throughout the night was impacted. I found that cannabis helped me fall asleep, but I did not feel rested in the morning. As I started to do the work to shift my perspective and heal, I also made sure my sleeping environment was nurturing and inviting. I decluttered and put up a soothing painting on the wall in front of my bed. I now have candles and incense handy in case I decide I would enjoy a calming scent before bed. I no longer turn on the lights in the house as the sun sets. After sundown, I let my eyes adjust to the dark, and this helps me wind down from the hustle and bustle of the day. During the winter months, when the sunset is earlier in the day, I occasionally turn on a dimmed light or candle, but only when I am doing something that requires some light, like reading or cooking.

When I am on a screen after sundown, I have a night filter on, and I tend to end screen time at least one hour before bed. At this time, I go to the bedroom and listen to music, meditate, or spend present time with Jason or the doggies. I almost always fall asleep within an hour, often within a few minutes. When I choose to listen to an audiobook or podcast before bed, I carefully choose the content I will consume during this time. If the content is super engaging or thought-provoking, it can keep me up.

Ignoring my phone and fighting boredom or my wandering mind has been a challenge. It's getting EASIER, but it's not easy. I found myself deeply conditioned to reach for my phone for every little question or thought. I have shut down the notifications on my phone, but the ones that pop up in my head are still very much on blast. But again, I love where I am on this journey, and it's not about being perfect; it's about retraining my mind and forming new habits.

Of course, our bodies and minds need more than just activity and rest to thrive. What we put into and onto our bodies also plays a key role in our overall health and well-being. I spend a lot of time each day thinking about **food**. Nowadays, I think about food in healthy ways. I plan ahead so I have something nutritious to eat when I become hungry. But this was not always the case. Any yummy thing that I craved seemed to be a push of a button away. Over the past decade, the world around me has changed, and with it, mindless habits have formed in my life. I used to travel for work quite often. This meant I didn't have access to a kitchen or always have time to buy groceries. Instead, I would eat out with friends or order food to be delivered to me. When I got back home from my travels, because I lived close to a major city and I was financially in a place where the cost of food or other consumables had become less of a worry, I started chasing comfort and convenience. Everyone around me was talking about all the cool new apps where you push a button, and magic happens. Taking the bus to work was replaced with a convenient Uber or Lyft ride. Food from miles away would magically appear at my door within thirty minutes. I wasn't eating fast food. I was ordering meals that were relatively healthier, so it was okay, right? But how often was I eating because it was time to eat or because I simply wanted to eat, as opposed to actually being hungry or needing food? How often were those large food portions ending up in my belly instead of leftovers to be enjoyed later? Not to mention the environmental impact.

Jason and I both knew how toxic this pattern was, and we talked openly about needing to do things differently, but every night when we got off work and walked the dogs, dinner was at our doorstep when we got home. In the world around me, seeking comfort and convenience has been normalized. If we did not participate, it felt like we were resisting the inevitable, like those people who held out on buying a TV when it was first invented or cell phones. Eventually, everyone would be using these tools, so what was the point of resisting? But the stories we tell ourselves matter because, as long as I held this perspective, there was no room for change. Jason's world was different than mine. Instead of working in the tech space, where life is all about efficiency, he obtained degrees in biology, natural resources, and nutrition. He has spent much of his life in school learning about how our bodies work and how to take care of them. His world is filled with people who value whole, healthy living over productivity and profit. He would share what he learned with me on a regular basis, but he was usually met with an eye roll or sarcastic comment about him not understanding my reality and perspective when, in fact, it was me who was not listening with the intention to learn and understand.

Over time, as I began my journey of living a more aware and present life, I saw this unhealthy consumption pattern more clearly. But even after seeing the pattern and the perspective it offered, it was hard to change. I would make the intention to change, and I would do my best to stay mindful, and yet when dinner time came around, I would still fall right back into the pattern less often than before but still more often than not. The only thing that had really changed was my comfort level with this behavior. Now, I was shaming myself for it because I knew better.

I read an excellent book about health and nutrition called "How Not To Die" by Dr. Michael Greger and Gene Stone. Dr. Greger is the founder of nutritionfacts.org. An organization made up of scientists and researchers who have dedicated their time to following nutrition and health studies around the world, validating their efficacy and sharing what they learn in an easy-to-understand and honest way. They are also quick to add or correct when new research provides additional or new information. They are in no way financially or otherwise tied to influential industries that bend reality for profit, so I have found them to be a good resource.

Jason, who had recommended this book to me, started making lifestyle changes around both what we put into and onto our bodies. He started buying hygienic and cleaning supplies that were more gentle on our bodies and the environment. He took over grocery shopping and prepped meals for himself so he could have better control over what he ate. He tried to include me, but I was not ready. I would participate to an extent, but I did not care about myself or the topic of healthy living enough to take the hard steps I had to take to change. Over the past five years, as I processed and released past trauma and started to gain a wider perspective on life, I have adopted many lifestyle changes, among them spending more time in the kitchen and less time on my phone.

I have learned that I love to cook and make food that tastes and looks good. I love to have friends over to share a meal, and I very much love to cook with Jason. We play some music, and we each take on a few tasks. I will chop while he stirs, or he will rinse the vegetables while I preheat the oven and prep the roasting pan. The food we make is simple, and we don't spend hours in the kitchen. We try to eat from the rainbow with both cooked and raw fruits and vegetables to accompany the delicious grains, beans and legumes, and nuts and seeds in our meals. We mostly eat plant-based foods, but not exclusively. Sometimes, it's hard to eat super healthy when traveling, so we just do our best to make mindful choices while also enjoying local foods and culture. I'm grateful for Jason's persistence. What was once a point of contention in our relationship has blossomed into beautiful life lessons and fulfilling new lifestyle norms.

One change I am working on now is being more present when I eat. Its easy to just eat while we watch a show together or eat fast to move onto whatever we want to do next, but I am learning that slowing down and taking the time to experience the smells and tastes of the food is a beautiful experience that I want to be present for. So now we sometimes eat at the table, or if the weather is pleasant, we will sit outside to eat. We also have limited eating after 7 pm. It's been a good practice for us not to surrender to late-night cravings. Its more of a choice to take care of our bodies and minds than a rule we feel obligated to follow. All of this is a choice. As long as we can manage to be aware and present, we get to choose what we buy, what we cook, what we eat, how much we eat, when we eat, and when we don't.

What are some ways that you provide activity, rest, and nutrients to your body? In what other ways do you nurture your body?

Now that we have discussed the areas of mind and body, let's talk about **connection**. There are many ways to thrive in our connections. The three ways that I will cover here are connection to other people through community building, connection to our planet and environment, and spiritual connection to something bigger than ourselves.

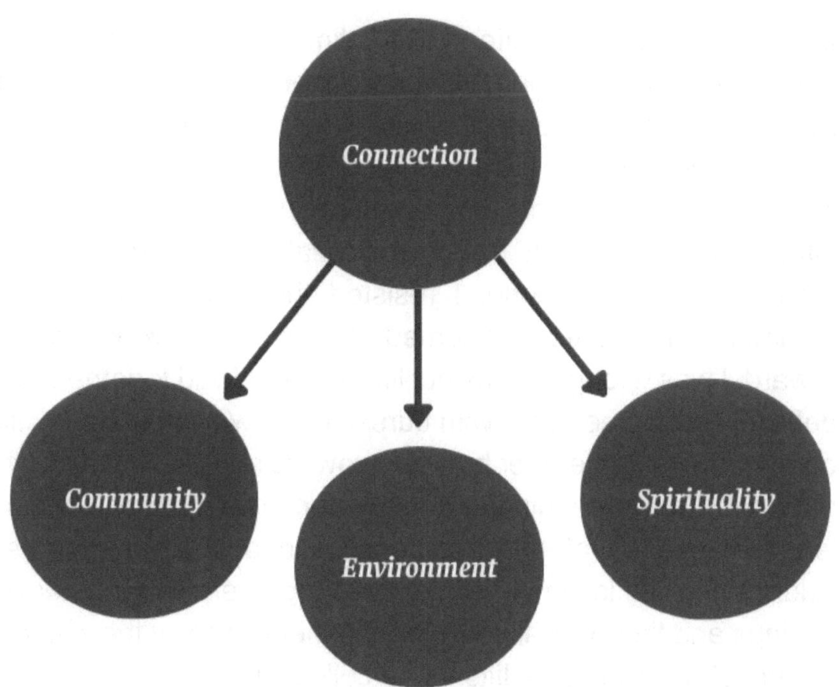

Let's start with **community**. Even though we live alongside eight billion other humans, in many parts of our society, it has been normalized to isolate. Our expectations of others have filled us with judgement to the point where we limit our interactions and when we do interact, we mostly have some version of a mask or wall in between the real vulnerable version of ourselves and others. We take on the labels of introversion and extraversion and like most labels we use, they put us in black and white boxes. If I am an introvert, that means I recharge when not around people, so that would mean my preference is to mostly be alone. If I am an extrovert, then I fill up with energy when around others, so I may find myself socializing even when I feel like I am running on empty. Instead of checking in with my mind and body, I now become a reactive product of a defined societal pattern.

For most of my adult life, I wore the crown of introversion. Sometimes, this label gave me an excuse to skip out on events that I was expected to attend. Sometimes it meant that I had a hard time fitting in when I did participate because it was so much work to be around people. Now, my perspective has shifted. I am not introverted or extraverted. I am human. And like all humans, I need time to myself to rest and do some introspective work, AND I need socialization because life is not meant to be lived alone. I resisted the idea of building a community for years. It seemed like so much work without reward. I was wrong. It turns out life is easier lived together. We definitely each need time with ourselves so we can learn to still our minds and remember how to be aware and present. But we also need real, meaningful social interaction so that we can learn from each other's perspectives and lifestyle choices. Additionally, life is simply easier lived together. Sharing heavy feelings and thoughts allows others to help us carry the weight. In turn, sharing our joys lifts us up collectively.

I still very much enjoy my own company and that of the members of my household. But my life has changed and expanded in the most beautiful way as I have learned to share my true self with others and create a safe, non-judgmental space for others to do the same with me. As part of this, I had to challenge things that had been normal to me before. I was taught to be independent and not ask for help. I felt I had to figure it out all on my own. Much like being compassionate, asking for help was often seen as a weakness in my world. But, like being compassionate, I found seeking assistance to be a source of strength. It takes courage to identify what you need and reach out for help, knowing there is a possibility of rejection. In my case, I would convince myself that I would be a burden in some way. As I challenged these thought patterns and set aside my fear, I learned that most people actually enjoy helping each other. It feels good to help someone. Pain stings less when shared. Laughter sounds louder when multiplied. Having real looks into each other's lives, also provides us with a sense of connectedness and we feel less lonely. After all, as humans, we are much more similar than we are different. What would happen if we started to look for relatable similarities instead of polarising differences in our interactions with others?

A few years ago, I had only a couple of friends, and the nature of these relationships was superficial to some extent. We had some shared interests but would never really talk about the deep stuff happening in our minds or bodies. I remember sharing a story about an argument I had with Jason with a friend and how I was feeling. She looked at me and said something to the effect of, I am sorry. I could tell she was also going through some issues with her partner at the time, but she didn't share much. I asked her how they were doing, and she gave me a short response about her partner having work to do to grow, implying she did not. Since I was being vulnerable about areas in which both Jason and I had to grow at the time, I felt a bit judged and unsafe to continue sharing. So we went right back to sharing just the superficial things in our lives. Every now and then, I would get glimpses of their real lives from the comments their kids would make, but nothing real from them directly. It felt shameful to talk about life struggles and relationship problems. It felt like we all had to pretend we had it all figured out. So, I pulled away over time and found myself with no friends at all. This felt fine, and I didn't feel the need to have friends, but of course, this was one of those “you don't know what you don't know” kinds of things.

Then I met Dawn. Dawn was a co-worker that I interacted with at work on occasion, and she was always a social ball of energy. She was all smiles and talked to anyone who would engage with her. I enjoyed talking to her at work, but I also always felt like I was late for something and felt bad for cutting her off and running to my next meeting. We were very different. I was reserved and mostly quiet. She was loud and almost always had a big, beautiful smile on her face. After I left the company, she and I stayed in touch and hung out a few times. She was the most real person I had ever met. She shared everything that was happening in her life—in her mind and in her body—freely, without any filters, at least from what I could tell. She was unapologetically human, and I was hooked. When she hugged me, she didn't give me an awkward half-second side hug. She hugged my entire existence with her entire being. She held me tight until I felt nurtured and safe, and only then would she give me a kiss on the cheek as she let me out of her loving arms. This was not a sexual attraction kind of thing, more like a sisterly connection.

I felt safe, loved, and seen by Dawn. She shared everything about her life freely, and I also felt safe to do so. At the time, I was in a weird toxic cycle in my mind where I could only see my ugly parts. What I was doing wrong or not doing but should have been doing. I had a myriad of expectations for myself and the world around me, and I was drowning in shame, judgement and fear, with no perspective to see that this was the case. When Dawn talked to me or about me, the way she would describe me was different. It's like she didn't see the crazy Type-A control freak who was awkward in her social interactions. Instead, she saw someone who was funny and kind, who talked to animals, and who enjoyed cooking with love. So, she nurtured and celebrated these parts of me. She would come over and share her perspective on things I did or said that would bring her joy. I slowly started to see myself differently. My perspective widened and now included how Dawn saw me. I slowly started to realize I could choose how to see myself as long as I was paying attention and not on autopilot. I was no longer defined by the rigid lines I had drawn for myself.

Dawn had a lot going on in her life at the time, but she always made time for me, and I looked at it as her doing me a service by being my friend. I remember her saying once that she felt badly for putting so much on me. It was in that moment that I realized the value of true human connection. We were sharing life together. We were carrying each other's heavy stuff, making it lighter to carry. We were also celebrating each other's joys, adding more joy to each of our own lives. Sharing life made it easier and more enjoyable.

Through Dawn, I met John, and John and I became instant besties. John was learning life lessons similar to mine. Specifically, spiritually, we understood each other. He understood my craziness, and I understood his. We immediately felt less alone, being able to talk about spiritual experiences and observations that we each had. He was also on the path of lowering his ego and was open to giving and receiving direct feedback. So, we challenged each other and grew through this friendship. I had never experienced anything like this before. This world had other humans in it that were willing to share their deepest inner thoughts, strengths, and shortcomings. Humans who were striving to be authentically humble and vulnerable as they quenched their thirst for life's delicious lessons. I found these relationships to be nurturing and rewarding, so it felt less like work and more like joy to maintain and build on these connections. My friendships with Dawn and John were my first real taste of community outside of family or career.

I started to understand what friendship and community meant. These people didn't come with the same stories as me; they had their own stories. They didn't share the same beliefs and worldview as me; they had their own conditioning to challenge and grow through and hardships to heal from. They added value to my life, and I did to theirs. Life was easier carried together. We felt lifted and supported by these relationships. That is what I understand community to be. A group of people who you feel safe and loved with and who challenge you compassionately to be your best self while also fully accepting and loving you as you are, bad choices and all. A group of people to live life with.

Like working on the mind, and taking care of the body, making and maintaining genuine connections takes effort. I set reminders for myself to text Dawn, John and others, often simply to let them know I am thinking of them, to give them a random life update, or to check in with them on something that was big for them at the time. This effort, though it felt more effortless than effortful, was returned in kind. They cared about me. They took the time to tell me how they felt, check in with me, and share about their lives. A simple "thinking of you and sending love" text went such a long way.

Once my community had a solid foundation, I decided I wanted to add to it carefully. I had a limited amount of time. Some time was dedicated to work. Time to take care of my body and mind. And some time to strengthen my relationship with Jason. So, I felt that I had to be intentional about how much time remained and how much of that I wanted to direct toward building community and in what ways. I decided to take advantage of the interconnectedness of these areas. What could I do that would allow me to spend time working toward a stronger relationship with Jason, would help me build community, and would nurture my mind and body? Jason and I both love plants and animals, so we started volunteering at various animal sanctuaries and environmental services. We pulled weeds and planted greenery. We maintained trails, took care of and made friends with feathered creatures. We built structures and demolished others. And through these experiences, we met new people. People that shared some of our values. We invited some over for shared meals and went on hikes with others. And just like that, my community expanded with beautiful new friends.

Not everyone we met was a good fit for us, or us for them. But some became a beautiful extension of our friend group and the closest of friends. We found our shared passion for music as we participated in and hosted what we call jam sessions, where everyone brings over a drum, rattle, handpan, ukelele or instrument of choice, and we make music just for fun. This time spent together is not about showing off our skills or competing. It's simply to be present with each other in joy. We all have different skill levels, and all sound is welcome. Some make bird noises with their mouths, while others shake a rattle or pluck a string. It's not about the performance or technicality of what is being shared. It's simply for fun. It's been wonderfully heartwarming and satisfying to just exist together and let our inner children bang and clank around as we learn to harmonize and create magic. Its been quite interesting getting to know other people and also meeting parts of ourselves that have been dormant, waiting to be discovered.

Another lovely byproduct of building community has been learning from other partners. Hearing about their struggles and sometimes seeing firsthand how they overcome disagreements and misalignments. Jason and I have been learning how to more effectively talk to and listen to each other. More directly, but also more compassionately. We have had our assumptions challenged by friends, making it easier to hear the feedback. We flow better together, and I am so grateful to our community for teaching us how to show up better for each other. I believe we have also influenced change in others. We all grow collectively by widening our realities through our very real discussions and interactions.

One thing I wish I had known earlier on this journey was that there is value in telling people around me what I am working on and that I am open to their feedback. Of course, this also means that I have to actually be open to listening to their feedback without getting defensive or argumentative. I don't have to take their feedback in its entirety or at all, but there is value in hearing others' perspectives about me or situations I face. They may give me a thread to pull on one of my patterns. Or I may not be ready for it or decide not to give weight to their feedback. I have found that receiving feedback gives me the opportunity to choose what I do with it.

Do you have people in your life that you can be fully vulnerable with while feeling safe and loved? Do you create a nonjudgmental space for others to feel safe around you? Are there friendships in your life that are unhealthy that maybe you want to revisit? In what ways can you make an effort to enhance your current relationships or build new ones?

But human connections are not the only connections that are needed for us to live full, healthy lives. Connection to our **environment** is an integral part of being human. We come from this planet and are connected to it not just by our need for air, water, and food but also by our relationships with plants, animals and our environment at large. The Big Bang happened roughly fourteen billion years ago; one billion years later, our galaxy was formed; another nine billion years passed, and our solar system came together. About a billion years after that, life started on our planet in the form of microscopic organisms. Then, in the past few billions of years, life evolved and went through a few mass extinctions until we arrived at this place. Our place in space and time. We humans came into existence, like all other life, as part of the energy of the universe. We also exist on a planet that also comes from that same energy. Why does this matter? Well, because when we try to separate ourselves from the rest of life on this planet, we tend to lose connection with something that is critical to our existence.

As I entered adulthood and life got busy, I mostly lost my connection to the natural world. At the same time, my mind would spin with recurring thoughts of shame and fear, and I would feel overwhelmed often. Though it wasn't until I read through past journals that I connected the dots between my connection to the environment and my mental health. Each time, as I reconnected with the trees and birds on the trails and the waters of the streams, lakes and waterfalls, I found that I was more in control of the thoughts and feelings that I observed in this body. I was more present and noticed more of what was happening around me and in me, which made those times in my life more meaningful. When I am around plants and animals, I am more easily able to calm my mind. Over the course of my life, I have remembered over and over again to enjoy the journey itself, as opposed to chasing a destination, each time becoming more present and pausing long enough to enjoy the many gifts around me. This was fascinating because, while it seems obvious afterwards, prior to this discovery, I was doing this more out of instinct than intention.

I have found both human and non-human life to be excellent teachers. Like us, non-human life has basic needs like food, water, sex, and sleep. But also, like us, they thrive when they feel safe and loved. Outside of these basic needs, you never see a bear worried about how they look or a hummingbird worried about what someone else's perception of their value is. They simply exist and try to have their needs met. When their needs are met, they have fun and play. They also act based on instinct and desire. We have evolved with the ability to be aware and to choose. So this also means we can choose which instincts to follow and which to challenge. For example, we evolved with a fear of scarcity so that we would hunt and gather food so we could continue to survive. Now, we live in houses and have more than we need and there is a grocery store around the corner from most of us, so that instinctual fear is instead driving us to overconsume and hoard. We catastrophize simple thoughts when we feel fear and worry. Leading to us making bad instinctual decisions as opposed to mindful and aware decisions that would benefit us and other life on earth.

In the spirit of connecting deeper with our environment, over the past years, Jason and I have brought many plants into our home. They bring us joy, and we take great care of them. Jason waters them and makes sure they have the right nutrients to thrive. I clean off their leaves and sing to them. And we change their soil together on an annual basis. We have also adopted two dogs that we love infinitely and try to express that love to them by spending fully present time with them, talking to them, and paying attention to what they are sharing as we learn from their communication patterns.

When Loki wants a neck rub, he comes up to me and puts his paw on my leg and looks down, so that I can rub his neck and cheeks as he nestles his head between my knees. When its dinner time, if I am not paying attention to the time, he comes up and grabs my attention, then walks me to the closet where his food is, and he repeatedly points to it with his nose and eyes, periodically looking back at me to see if I understood. When Loki is sore from a hike and needs a massage, he comes up to me and sniffs his legs while looking up at me and breathing calmly but loudly. If his knee or hip is inflamed and sensitive to touch, he sniffs the painful area and breathes rapidly without making eye contact with me. This lets me know he wants me to avoid this area when touching him. Consent has also created a sweet bond between us. When I want to snuggle with Loki, I go up to him and ask him if he is good with touch, and I hold the palms of my hands up in front of his face. If he puts his face in my palms and wags his tail, that is a yes. If he turns his head away and his tale does not move, that is a no. He has a choice in the matter, and it has been beautiful to build this kind of trust in my relationship with him.

On days when we don't have time for a whole hike, we go to a short trail or park nearby, or we drive somewhere to catch the sunset. And, of course, there is kayaking, which has become a favorite of mine. Something about being out on the water and feeling so small in the significance of it all is magic—a beautiful reminder not to take myself too seriously. Maintaining a small garden and volunteering have been some of the other ways I have become more deeply connected with non human friends.

In what ways are you connecting with our beautiful planet and non-human life around you? What are some ways you can connect more often and more deeply?

Building and strengthening connections with human and non-human life over the past few years, has brought an abundance of joy to my life. One other very unexpected connection for me has been a connection to **spirituality**. Our spiritual beliefs seem to be tied to our perspective and reality, so how we even define spirituality can be vastly different from person to person. So, I won't attempt to generalize what it means or how to arrive at it, as your journey will undoubtedly be different than my own. Instead, I will share what spirituality is for me at this moment in time.

At thirty-seven-years old, I had been an atheist for as long as I remember having an opinion on the matter. I always felt religion was something that was pushed on me at school or through society. At home, I had the influence of Mamanee's progressive reading habits. I had learned about many religions and belief systems, and by my late teens, I had become rigidly and judgmentally opposed to joining what I called one cult over another. I didn't believe in anything outside of what seemed to be reasonably factual from my perspective. I have been an avid follower of science, so if science did not explain something, odds were there was no room for it in my world.

After my experiences with plant medicines, as well as various breathwork and meditation practices, I found myself experiencing things that were reasonably factual in a whole new way, outside of what has been explained with science. At first, I chalked up what was happening to hallucinations and coincidences. I would have a vision or thought during meditation or in a dream, and then a few days later, what I had seen in my vision would come to pass. Hallucinations and coincidences. As I became more aware and present, this started happening more and more, so I started writing down what and when I had experienced these visions or thoughts. It turns out that if something happens enough times, it's hard to chalk it up to a coincidence. Still, I continued to shut myself off from the possibility of spiritual expansion. Even now, as I write this, I am having internal discussions with myself back and forth about how I am becoming woo-woo and convincing myself of things that could not possibly be true outside of fairytales and sci-fi. Yet, I have experienced things that have given me a connection to something bigger than myself.

Believing in the possibility of there being a lot more than what we experience through our main senses of sight, hearing, smell, taste and touch is an interesting thought. Through science, we know that the diversity of life on this planet experiences life in different ways based on the frequencies they hear or the wavelengths they see. We do not all share the same senses nor are our dominant senses the same across the board. Even how we communicate is unique to each of our species. Additionally, studying the human body, much like studying our planet, is a beautiful testament to the connectedness of all things. A great many things have to align for us to have food to eat. A greater number of things need to align in our bodies and environment for that food to be absorbed, digested, filtered, and expelled in ways that are healthy. The point being that all things are connected and we as humans living in this place in space and time only experience a small subset of these connections due to the limitations of our bodies and further limited by societal norms limiting our minds.

I don’t currently believe in a god or gods or any flavor of heaven or hell. I don't know what happens when we die or if reincarnation is a thing. I also don't believe that anyone living in this life knows for sure what happens after. But I do believe we all come from the energy of the universe and when we die, that energy goes back into the universe, whether it be as potential dormant energy or kinetic energy in one way or another, somewhere in space and time. Whether that belief is accurate or not, its fun to think about, and it has added value to my life without having harmful side effects. It’s allowed me to release the idea of being good in pursuit of some kind of reward and just simply strive to show up well because I can. It’s allowed me to see all human and non-human life as an extension of myself, allowing me to seek to understand their perspective and compassionately love them as best I can. So this belief system is working well for me. I have no intention of trying to convince anyone that my way is THE way or that their way is wrong. That is ego-based thinking and, in my opinion, irrelevant. I find living this life in this body pretty cool, and the fact that our human brains have evolved to be able to have these types of thoughts is completely fascinating. This perspective brings me joy, and it is about just that for me. It's about feeling connected, whole and happy.

We are all here to figure out how to do life, and life is easier and better when we are kind and as close to expectation-free as we can be. Experience has taught me that life is better when we are aware, present and mindful of our choices. Life is better when we show up for each other and ourselves, not because we have to but simply because we can. Life is better when we learn from and release our stories, as opposed to hoarding them and punishing ourselves with recurring suffering. Life is better when we notice the magic around us and share gratitude for all the things that make this very life possible.

As my life became easier with this new belief system, more and more I realized that life is not about me. All the things I would worry about and get caught up in were just constructs in my mind that led to suffering. It turns out that life is not about me at all, but rather about life itself. Its not about me as an American or Iranian person. Its not about me as a woman. Its not about me as a person of color or pan queer individual. Its about us as a collective. Its about taking responsibility for how we show up, serving life itself and taking care of each other and our planet. Its about learning how to reside on this fun little rock at this random point in this vast universe in a way that looks different than how we mindlessly live today.

When we live better, choose better, and love deeper, magic happens. I have experienced things that I never would have imagined possible. I was walking on a trail last summer with Loki and Jason and we came across a horse and his rider. We stepped to the side to let them pass and as I made eye contact with the horse and smiled, he nodded. Then he walked up to me, despite his riders pull, and put his forehead on mine, closing his eyes and exchanging what I received as his feelings and love. I have never rode a horse or been around horses but looking into this horse's eyes, I felt connected to him and seen by him. That was magic and that is what spirituality is to me.

Two years ago, while backpacking, I decided to stay behind at camp and do some wood carving while Jason and our friend walked a short trail nearby. I was singing, as I do when I'm alone, and some birds gathered. One of them started singing with me and was brave enough to hop closer and closer until they were sitting on my barefoot, rubbing their cheek on my ankle. That was magic and that is what spirituality is to me. More and more, I feel an exchange of energy and feelings as I touch animals and plants on my adventures. There is magic all around me and I feel spiritually connected, not just to life on this planet but to energies beyond this life. I have had exchanges with beings I have no labels for. These beings have guided me and provided me with advice, knowledge and power. Again, my goal here is not to convince anyone of anything. I am just vulnerably sharing what has been true for me, knowing most of you will slap a crazy label on it as I would have just a few years ago.

What are some ways you feel spiritually connected? Are spirituality and religion intertwined in your reality? Is your belief system unlocking your potential for compassion or reinforcing societal norms of hording shame and passing judgment far and wide?

So now we have talked about the areas of mind, body and connection, as well as the lifestyle choices and perspective shifts that can help us on this journey of healing, growth, and fulfillment. As we embark on this journey and receive the gift of joy through gratitude and inner peace through a calm mind and a healed inner child, we then face the question of: What is the purpose of all of this? Why am I here?

As I started to make changes to my life over the past years, my ocean of life has cleared, and I have found countless new ways to serve. What was once a heavy question is now a fun little game. Like much else in my life, I was very much overthinking what our purpose is as humans in this place in space and time. Could it be that its as simple as serving? Serving life. Serving kindness. Serving eachother. The basic idea here is that as we heal, we find that we have many gifts. Some that we excel at, some newly discovered and developing, and some yet to be found. These gifts, be it playing an instrument, singing, organizing, building something, taking care of others, growing food, etc., are our contribution to life.

After leaving my job and taking six months off, I went back into the tech space, working as the Vice President of Strategy and Operations at a small startup. I spent the following two years leading in a new way that was more present and compassionate, in alignment with the lessons I had been learning during this time. I developed genuine connections with incredible people and I had so much fun sharing stories and carrying life with them. I both inspired and was inspired by these connections and when I left, I found myself busier than when I was formally working. Friends and friends of friends started to reach out to me for advice and guidance on their own paths to fulfillment.

I have found that I thoroughly enjoy this work and this very much feels like one of those purposeful sunrays in my ocean of life. So now, among other things, I am also a life coach, a career coach and an immigration adaptation coach. I spend my days connecting with people and sharing stories and knowledge as we learn from each other. I work with refugees from war or other hardship who are adapting to life in the United States. I work with folks at a variety of stages in their careers looking to grow their skills, lead well, or serve in ways inside of or outside of their career. I also work with fulfillment seekers on their healing and growth journeys. I am learning that I can serve purpose not only in my job but also in community gatherings and interactions with people whom I have just met. I can serve by sharing what I have learned, by creating a safe space for others to share, by learning from others stories, by sharing art and music with the world, by caring for others and by sharing my strength. There are endless ways for me, and all of us, to serve many purposes by how we show up in this life. I am so grateful to be living a life that leaves me thinking, “How is this my life and how am I so lucky?” every night before I put my head down and every morning when I wake up.

I hope that my story, if nothing else, put an occasional smile on your face. What is your story and how has it changed as your perspective continues to widen? Have you provided your inner child with the safety and love they need to heal and join you on this full little journey we call life? What kind of impression do you leave on those you interact with? What are some lifestyle changes that you can make to live a more simple and fulfilling life? How are you showing up in life and what lessons have you learned? In what areas are you still actively challenging yourself to grow? Do you accept yourself and love yourself as you are today? In what ways do you share your power and inspire those around you to live life better?

compassion, deep within us

we call on you

wisdom, deep within us

we call on you

power, deep within us

we call on you

we surrender

expectations

judgement

and guilt

we surrender

fears

and sense of self

awake and aware, we breath

awake and aware, we breath

connected and empty, we serve

Acknowledgements

My most sincere gratitude to Andy Fischer Price for the magic he brings to this world through his music and words. You have inspired awareness and presence in me, and for that, I will forever be grateful.

To my beautiful friends Nora and Micah Heath, who walk the path of love and compassion and spread sunshine especially during times when the heavy in life is extra heavy.

To the creative and talented Jon Hanzelka for bringing my healed inner child to life on the cover of this book. I am blown away by the love and detail you express through your art.

I have been so blessed to meet countless people who walk the path of life with grace and humility, shining light on ways to show up well in life. Thank you for the guidance, inspiration, and love. My life is forever changed.

Made in United States
Troutdale, OR
11/06/2024

24494853R00106